Tune in to your
Spiritual
Potential

If our minds are focused upon the earth, we will pay little attention to the spiritual dimension of life. But if our lives are centred in the realisation of the Spirit, the earth will seem transient and the Spirit will be seen as the dominant force working in and through all things.

This book is dedicated to the memory of
Rosetta Margaret Wollaston
and Gordon M. Higginson.

The authors wish to thank Julie Friedeberger,
Jean Matheson and Swami Dharmānanda Saraswati.
Without their help, support, encouragement and
friendship, this book would not have been possible.

Tune in to your Spiritual Potential

Glyn Edwards and Santoshan

quantum

LONDON • NEW YORK • TORONTO • SYDNEY

quantum

An imprint of W. Foulsham & Co. Ltd
The Publishing House, Bennetts Close, Cippenham, Slough,
Berkshire, SL1 5AP, England

ISBN 0-572-02510-6

Reflections from a Spiritual Notebook appears
by courtesy of the *Dharma Journal*.

Printed in Great Britain by St. Edmundsbury Press, Bury St. Edmunds, Suffolk.

Contents

Preface

Tune in to your Spiritual Potential is organised in three parts. Part One, *Ways*, gives guidance on various practices for spiritual growth. Part Two, *Attunement*, focuses on the psychic and mediumistic areas of development, and is intended to give the reader a practical understanding of them and how they function. Part Three, *Synthesis*, looks at personal development, and suggests ways in which we can awaken to qualities of the True Self, and attain a richer level of life and being. The two articles in Appendices One and Two have been included because they relate to material in this book.

At the end of each part, there are various exercises. There are also other exercises in some of the individual chapters. *Tune in to your Spiritual Potential* is essentially a workbook for those who wish to know more about all aspects of development. Observations are put forward in order to make clear what various exercises and practices are useful for, and what may or may not be expected through practising them.

Please note that where the word 'spirit' appears with a small 's' it refers to one's inner spirit or to individual spirit helpers and the world they inhabit. Spirit in this sense may be referred to in the plural – one may often hear mediums talk of 'the spirit and *their* influence'. Where a capital 'S' is used, it refers to the Supreme Spirit and represents a single reality. Similarly, Self may be written with a capital 'S' to denote one's higher, spiritual God-Self or with a small 's' to denote one's psychological self.

We hope the book will serve a purpose for its readers. If *Tune in to your Spiritual Potential* helps a few people a little further along the path to spiritual development, our efforts will have been rewarded. We wish you peace and many pleasant awakenings on your journey. May each day lead you closer to realising your full spiritual potential.

Glyn Edwards was born in Liverpool and has been a working medium for over 30 years. He entered a closed religious order at 16, which intensified his mediumistic abilities and led him back into the world. He has travelled extensively, speaking, lecturing, demonstrating and running workshops worldwide, and is a regular senior course tutor at Treysgawen Hall and at the Arthur Findlay College (a college for the study and advancement of psychic science). He has also worked at the Society for Psychical Research and the Spiritualist Association of Great Britain. He is a certificate holder of the Spiritualists' National Union, is listed in the *Best of British*, and has been involved with the research of PRISM (Psychical Research Involving Selected Mediums).

Glyn Edwards has also been interviewed on television and radio, has recorded many tapes, and has written numerous articles on psychic and mediumistic development.

Santoshan (Stephen Wollaston) was born and lives in London. He was initiated by Swami Dharmānanda Saraswati and has been a student of teachings from both East and West for over 20 years. He graduated from King's College, University of London, with a high honours degree in Religious Studies, and has trained in Transpersonal Counselling. He has written on Indian religions and spiritual development, and contributes regularly to the *Dharma Journal* (the quarterly magazine of the Dharma Yoga Centre). He has given talks on philosophy and transpersonal development and comparisons with mystical experience and Eastern wisdom, organised spiritual retreats and development courses, and was involved in the start of the Publicity and Public Relations Committee of the Spiritualists' National Union.

Santoshan also has a creative background as an artist, musician, graphic designer and graphics teacher, and is the founder and co-producer of the music group Sadhana.

Introduction

This book is a compilation of shared thoughts, observations and techniques, which we have found useful in our own search and development. The purpose of *Tune in to your Spiritual Potential* is not to add more concepts to people's understanding of spiritual matters, but to serve as a practical guide to various aspects of development which will, we hope, help individuals to become more open and receptive to spiritual growth.

In approaching mediumistic, psychic or spiritual development, there are no set rules to follow to reach a specific goal. There are only guidelines and pointers to the way ahead. It is up to each of us to decide which road we wish to take in order to find and make our own way along whatever path is best suited to our nature, and through that develop our awareness and take responsibility for our development. It is an ever-evolving process, which opens us to new experiences and leads us to a deeper understanding of life.

We should not put preconceived ideas upon how we wish to be used or influenced by God or the spirit world. It is best to watch patiently and see what unfolds, and leave ourselves open to their power and influence to bring forward whatever potential lies within.

This does not mean that our development should be passive or effortless, for our blending with that power should be a conscious activity – a mixture of concentration, awareness and receptivity. A half-hearted approach will achieve little, as our attitudes affect the way in which we develop. If we are narrow in our thinking, our development will be narrow. Conversely, if we are open and broad in our thinking, more areas of our lives will be receptive to development.

To be in tune with the spiritual dimension of life, there must be a letting go of our desires and any restrictive concepts that we may have. We have to surrender all notions of 'I', 'Me' and 'Mine' – anything that separates us from the sacred in *all* – and penetrate beneath the surface layers of our personality in order to become aware of the true Self and blend our consciousness more purely with the influence of God and spirit. The more this can be done, the finer our spiritual perception will be.

Learn to stand aside and be open to direction and guidance. Seek God and the spirit on their terms and you will develop in ways you may not have realised you had the potential for. Development is about change. We might notice our lives becoming fuller and more meaningful. Things that used to annoy us may do so no longer. We may become more accepting, peaceful, positive and compassionate, and more openly expressive.

This should not isolate us from the natural world, but instead give us renewed vigour to face up to life, and to live it with our feet planted firmly on the ground. It should give us the courage, strength and confidence to be true to life and our living of it.

Spiritual growth means taking any practices we are following (affirmations, prayer, meditation, etc.) into the outside world and learning to live the spiritual life in the midst of all things, no matter how difficult or busy our lives may be. It means striving to live one's life by the ideal of 'living in the world, without being inhibited by it'. If we are able to touch and manifest the spiritual side of our personality only in times of quiet, inactive solitude, then what use are we to anyone? What good can we contribute? Remember that it is often in times of trouble that a truly spiritual person is needed.

If you feel you require more time or peace in your life before setting out on the spiritual path, you are missing the point. Start where you are, with any problems you have, and develop from there. For development is closely related to how we use our time. A complex life, which places too much value on worldly activity, will leave little room for observing spiritual precepts or practices, whereas learning how to transform whatever is unnecessary in our lives can give us the time we need for development, and reveal a fuller, simpler and more harmonious way of living.

But development does not lie in solving every problem that may confront us, but in growing beyond the things that might appear to block our progress. Through this, various entanglements can be avoided. We may not be able to change the world but we can at least change ourselves.

The time to start out on this path is now, as it is what we do with our lives in the present that is most important. The past has gone and can never be changed; only our response to it can. But the present can hold many possibilities. All we have to do is be open and receptive to positive growth, willing to become more perfect instruments for the work of the Infinite Spirit.

PART ONE

Ways

Be mindful, open and compassionate.

Word P

Lead me from the visible to the mm.
Take me from the shadow into light.
Teach me how to attune my life with Thine.

We should not underestimate the power of words in our development, as language is the most powerful gift that we have. Words have the capacity to express our innermost feelings: they can unite or divide nations and express pure unconditional love, or hatred and bitterness.

If one person were to speak harshly to another, the abused person might feel a sense of outrage at being treated unjustly, and his or her emotions would suddenly change – even if only one harsh word were spoken. So if just one word can have such an adverse effect and give rise to negative emotions, we must also consider what use words can have for positive use and growth.

It is no coincidence that the many spiritual traditions of the world have adopted various uses of prayer, chant, mantra and affirmation. Each can affect and help us in a different way; each has its own value if used correctly. They all provide a way of transcending everything that denies the spirit that we are, so that we centre our awareness in the truth of our being. As we pray or chant, we reflect on the Spirit and eventually become absorbed in the Spirit's presence.

The psychology of chants, mantras and affirmations

In the Far East, chants and mantras have long been recognised as important aids in spiritual development. In fact, every word we use and every thought we have is a kind of mantra. We are constantly feeding our unconscious with words and thoughts that produce different results, as our conscious mind affects the unconscious level of our being, and our unconscious mind affects the conscious level of our being.

We might pay little attention to something and have little

it. Therefore it will have little hold over us. On the other
may have an experience to which we react quite strongly and
ly. In this case, it can have a lasting effect upon us. (We can also
ected by events unconsciously.) But as explained above, it is not just
the conscious level that we are affected, as every experience is
recorded by the unconscious, which in turn influences the conscious
mind. It is a never-ending cycle, which if we are not careful, can become
more and more negative and lead us further away from awakening our
spiritual consciousness.

The more negative experiences we feed in, the more negative our
character can become, and the more negative our reactions can be. Yet
if we keep the conscious mind actively focused upon the positive nature
of Spirit whilst praying, chanting or using an affirmation, we can
transform our overall nature and draw creative strength from the infinite
Source of all.

The power of chants, mantras and affirmations

Chants, mantras and affirmations give us a tool to creatively change our
level of awareness. They help us stop our conscious minds behaving so
erratically. They also help us keep our minds focused upon an aspect of
our true natures and cease the flow of negative reactions; so that we
become more positive and attract and develop attributes in harmony
with that vibration. Thus, we use the law of cause and effect creatively
to enhance our spiritual potential.

Chants and mantras have meaning as well as purpose. They are not
merely abstract sounds. The mantra *So Ham* (pronounced *Sah-Hum*)
means 'I Am That'. *Om* (pronounced *O-aum*) is said to be the first sound
that God created, from which all else was made. So if you meditate on
So Ham – which is practised by silently repeating *So* on the in-breath and
Ham on the out-breath – you will be meditating on the God within. If
you chant *Om*, you meditate on a sound that is said to have created all
life and to resonate throughout the universe: 'In the beginning was the
Word, and the Word was with God, and the Word was God'[1]. Some
mystics are said to have heard the sound of *Om* in certain states of
meditation.

Most mantras are positive statements that either affirm or surrender
to God's presence. Others represent vital sounds that vibrate within us

and the universe. If we wish to achieve benefit from these practices, we should be aware of their purpose, conscious of their particular sound and vibration resonating within ourselves as we use them.

Some may feel uncomfortable using a language or tradition different from their own, and be more at ease repeating the word *God* on the in- or out-breath, and through that focus their attention upon the Divine within. Others could find a phrase or sentence in their own language more helpful.

There are, of course, many types of chants, mantras and affirmations. Each serves a different purpose. You may want to try one word that has a quality you wish to develop, or use an affirmation that is more descriptive in helping you to recognise the spirit that you are. All can be of benefit in your development.

Affirmations for use in your spiritual journey

The following affirmations can be used in meditation or during your normal day. But do not repeat them at times when you should be giving your full attention to something else, such as driving a car or operating machinery:

I surrender to the spirit of the inner Self.

The spirit's direction is my direction.

I honour the Supreme Spirit in all life.

Using mantras

When you use a word or phrase in a repeated mantra form, create a rhythm between the word(s) and your breathing – repeating it once for every in- and out-breath. Breathe calmly and evenly, and repeat the word(s). First voice the mantra for a period of time to get used to the way it sounds. After a while repeat it silently, taking the sound and rhythm of the mantra within yourself. If you use one of the traditional yogic or Buddhist mantras, it is important to get the correct pronunciation and sound of the mantra so that it resonates properly within you.

17

When choosing a specific mantra as your main one (others can be used and changed as secondary mantras), it is advised that you retain it for use over a period of time – some say for life. Do not change it from week to week, but use the same one regularly in order to gain full benefit from it. Unlike some methods of meditation where a word which has a passive quality about it, such as 'peace', can be reflected upon, it is better to use something more specific that invokes the universal life force within you.

Tried and tested mantras are recommended, but seek expert advice before plunging yourself into an unfamiliar practice. Although the sound and vibrations of certain words can affect and awaken spiritual energies within us, it is advisable to seek professional advice from a qualified and recommended practitioner before trying more complex mantras or chants as you may awaken certain energies within yourselves before you are ready to handle them. It is for this reason that we have concentrated upon easy-to-use affirmations, instead of giving our readers something that may not be suitable for their development. If you wish to know more about mantras and how to use them, you will find four practical introductory books listed in the *Recommended Reading* at the end of this book.

The power of prayer

There are two kinds of spoken prayer: the affirmative and the kind that asks God and spirit to perform a particular act. With affirmative prayer, we have to be careful that it does not lead to self-glorification, as nothing could be further from the true purpose of spiritual development. We should be constantly on our guard against this happening.

What affirmative prayer should do is bring about a recognition of the unlimited creative spirit within us and within all life around us, and help us to surrender ourselves to that power and influence.

The other kind of prayer is often misunderstood and used with little result by many, who generally ask in a half-hearted and half-believing way for something to happen (usually to a power that is separate from themselves), while at the same time attaching themselves to the problem that confronts them, dwelling upon it and giving it more strength and power over them. Needless to say, this is not the ideal way to use prayer. Instead, look at prayer in these ways:

1   Before asking for the fulfilment of any worldly needs, we should first seek a wider perception of life, otherwise we may find that what we are praying for is of little help to our spiritual growth. We must first have practical knowledge of the nature of God and spirit. If we have limited ideas of our relationship to the spiritual laws that govern the universe, our practices will have limited results.

If we are to pray for anything, we should first ask for more spiritual understanding, in order to become more spiritually aware and to realise that we are not separate from God or spirit: we are all connected in the one complete whole and God's power works through everything.

2   There must be conviction in what we are doing. Why bother praying if we do not believe our prayers can have an effect? So cultivate a positive approach to prayer, have confidence that it works and is a means by which you can enhance your spiritual potential.

3   Leave things in the hands of God and spirit to do their work. Recognise that there is nothing that God and spirit cannot do. This does not mean that we should deny or suppress any problems that may confront us. Only by facing life and understanding what is going on beneath our surface consciousness can we make progress in our spiritual development. Any emotional blockages that we may be holding on to will have to be healed through a process of acknowledging that they are there, letting them in – giving them some space, feeling into and understanding what they are about – and accepting them. Only then can the final process of letting go and no longer identifying with them really begin.

4   Prayer has to be used to stimulate and enhance our development, and bring us to that point of recognising that *we too are spirit*, that *we too are part of God*, and give ourselves to that Power and allow it to manifest itself in us, as us. We do not deny the physical dimension of life, but instead affirm that it is Spirit in essence: the body exists because of its spiritual nature functioning through it and giving it life.

5   Strengthen your link with God and the spirit every day by making prayer a regular part of your development. *Do not wait until trouble strikes before you decide to do this.*

How prayer functions

The quality of our prayer will depend on our level of understanding and our ability to be in tune with the Infinite. The power of prayer is found in the way we say the words, whether mentally or verbally. If there is true feeling and compassion behind the words, as well as an attained level of awareness, our prayers will stimulate a deeper level of our being. The spirit in us, which is linked to the Spirit in all life, will recognise and respond to the meaning of our words and will bring about a corresponding result, using whatever channels are available to it. This is, in essence, what occurs in some forms of distant healing. Yet prayer and affirmation should be only the means to an end, and not the end in itself. It should lead us to that state of complete silence where we give ourselves to God and to spirit's power and influence so that they may work more freely in and through us. Through prayer and affirmation, we can focus our attention more strongly upon God and spirit, and in turn strengthen our awareness of our spiritual consciousness.

*   *   *

A personal realisation exercise

Be quiet and compose your thoughts. Make your link with the spirit, and find peace and strength in that contact. Affirm your relationship to the spirit world. Affirm your relationship to the Divine Reality that exists in all things and repeat the following affirmation:

> *I recognise the Supreme Spirit within me, and acknowledge*
> *my oneness with all life. All is in harmony with my life as*
> *I allow the creative power of the Spirit to flow freely in me*
> *and through me.*

Finish by 'dis-identifying' yourself from anything that creates the appearance of separation from this creative power, and by affirming that all these things are now done. 'Dis-identification' is a descriptive term used in psychosynthesis which means a person's ability to recognise a subpersonality and observe it objectively.

Directing Thought

Teach me how to co-operate with Your guidance,
and become rich in wisdom and understanding.

It is said that God is Spirit, and that both man and woman are also spirit, the same substance that is God. We are told that we live, move and have our being in a spiritual universe. But what can we do if we have not arrived at that level of prayer where we can discover this truth for ourselves?

First, we must realise that prayer is simply thought rightly directed. 'Directed where?' you may ask. If we go back to the first statement, that God is Spirit, and that man and woman are also spirit here and now, and possess within them some spark of the God-Spirit, it follows that for prayer to be effective, we must direct it first within ourselves and commune with the God that manifests as us. We should try and develop a sense of God and ourselves as being One, and lose any sense of being separate.

One way to proceed towards knowing this is to try to feel and sense this aspect while using words aloud, such as 'I know that God is within me as my own spirit, my own consciousness, my own eternity and my own creativity'. But what is more important than the method you use is that it starts to open and lead you to building a conscious relationship with God within, and open the creative principle within yourself. This can be achieved by using constructive words, thoughts and feelings.

As we know that thoughts are living entities in themselves, so, too, must our feelings and words be. That is why we must be selective in what we think, feel and say in prayer, because the creative principle, the law of cause and effect, will automatically come into operation.

First realise the God within you, and remember, you do not bargain with yourself, so do not bargain with the God within. Talk to God as you would to a friend or someone you love. Let your prayer be natural and express just how you feel. Open yourself up to God. As you do so, you will find yourself opening up to yourself. This is important as it will help you to be more self-aware and build a stronger bond between yourself and the Self that is God.

You can also use affirmations to keep your prayer alive and moving. Be positive about yourself and your relationship to God. Understand the true meaning of 'the presence of God', that we have qualities of God within us, and that It holds nothing back.

Practising affirmative prayer

Make a definite time, twice a day if possible, to be alone. Sit down and compose your mind and think about God. Try to arrive at a deep sense of peace and calm, then assume an attitude of trust in that Great Power that is God. Next say to yourself the following:

The words I speak express the law of goodness and will bring about positive growth, because they are operating on the creative power of God that is within me. Good alone goes from me, and good alone returns to me.

You are now ready to expand your positive affirmation. Begin by saying:

These words are for myself (speak your name). Everything I say is for me and about me. It is the truth about my real Self (think about your spiritual nature, the divine reality of yourself – the God in you).

I know that God is the eternal source of goodness, light, love, wisdom, truth and perfection. These attributes are mine now at this moment because these things of God are within me and God's creative power is within me. The God that is within me is the giver and sustainer of all life. I know that I (repeat your name) receive from this great power of goodness all that I need for my spiritual journey. My every need is met now (state your need).

I let go of all negative thoughts – I release them. I let go of all negative emotions – I release them. I let go of all doubts about myself and my pathway in life – I release them. I know that God and the spirit will guide and direct me to make the right decisions in my life. I give thanks, and so it is.

Statements such as this are not so much instructions to God, but are positive affirmations which remind us that God is limitless, and is expressing Itself as our individualised spirit, and expressing through us that self-same limitlessness. It is God's pleasure to give. The more open we are consciously to receive, the greater will be our capacity to receive. This all operates through the universal law of cause and effect. Look at it reasonably: 'As a man thinks, so he becomes'. This statement can be seen as true at every level of our being. If we are little-minded, we receive little in return. If we are loving, we will attract love. If we are hateful, we shall attract hate. Laughter attracts more laughter. Joy attracts more joy, and so on.

So let us be reasonable, realistic and honest with ourselves, and remember that it is God's good pleasure to supply without limit. Let us then be greater-minded that we may receive greater things.

Basic Steps

My life is one with my heart,
and my heart is full of loving kindness.

Until fairly recently the practice of meditation was looked upon as something mysterious, and the people who practised it were considered somewhat strange. Today the overall view of meditation has changed. Most people realise that it can be practised by anyone, and that we do not have to be particularly religious in order to benefit from practising it. There is no danger in meditation provided that the practitioner is of sound mental health and sensible in going about the practice.

Many have found meditation relaxing and of great help in today's stressful world. Certain types of meditation have proved to have remarkable results in calming the mind and relaxing the body. Yet these are only the fruits of meditation, not ends in themselves. The ultimate aim of meditation is to bring about a change in our perceptions as well as a change in our lives.

Preparation before meditation practice

Meditation plays a vital role in the development of mediumistic, psychic and spiritual awareness. A sound and practical understanding of it will give the practitioner a strong base on which to build.

If you have never practised meditation before, it is best to learn in a meditation class or quietly at home. If at home, unplug the phone, close the windows and pull the curtains to avoid the distractions of exterior noises or sudden bursts of sunlight or car headlights. In time you will find that these things will be less distracting.

Give yourself time to get into the right frame of mind. You may lead a busy life, but rushing into the practice and dashing off afterwards is an opportunity missed. Even if some benefit is gained, it will soon be lost. To slow down before or after a busy day, it helps to take some preliminary steps before you start:

1 Gather your thoughts before you meditate and bring to mind what you are about to do. Realise the importance of this time you have set aside. Leave all exterior thoughts and concerns aside.

2 Because certain sounds and vibrations can make us more receptive to blending with the spiritual dimension of our being, it can be beneficial to chant or listen to a soothing piece of music before meditating. Music can balance the creative and intellectual parts of the brain and enhance receptivity to intuition by bringing about a relaxed state.

You may at first find it helpful to use music during your meditation. As time goes on and you become more accustomed to meditating, it is best to limit the use of music purely to the preliminary stage of helping you relax and not during the meditation itself, as you might find your attention being drawn to the music instead of concentrating on your practice. Your mind might even start to conjure up images to fit the mood of the music. But it can be interesting to see how music affects you.

Basic sounds can also be used and projected out loudly into the air, such as, 'O-o-o-o', 'A-r-r-r', 'E-e-e-e', 'O-h-h-h', 'A-y-y-y', 'E-m-m-m' or 'E-n-n-n'. These have a relaxing and focusing effect on the mind and body. If you try this exercise, exhale slowly and gently, projecting and concentrating on the sounds. Be aware of their vibration within the body and within the air as you sound them. Repeat each sound five times.

3 The place in which you sit could have a picture (possibly of a spiritual teacher you admire) or some flowers that you find uplifting to look at beforehand. You might also wish to introduce an element of ritual into your practices by lighting a candle or some incense, arranging some flowers, or ringing a singing bowl or bell. All these can help detach your mind from daily activities and stir something of the spirit within.

4 It can help to read a short passage or two from a book that inspires you, something that reminds you of what you are striving to achieve in your period of meditation.

5 You may wish to affirm your oneness with God and spirit, or send out a prayer which asks for guidance in your practice.

None of these is compulsory, but they may help you focus your mind upon the purpose of meditating, take your attention away from the events of the day and help you to concentrate better.

A place to meditate

Upon entering a place of worship, you may have felt a strong silent presence surrounding you. This did not happen overnight, but developed over years through constant devotion and prayer, creating a conducive atmosphere for reflection upon God and the spirit. For this reason many prefer to set aside a room or place solely for the purpose of meditation. If this is not possible, then perhaps a special meditation cushion and mat or chair can be used, something that will not be used for any other purpose, or be associated with any other activity.

Posture

Wear loose-fitting clothing or loosen any tight clothing, as this will help you relax and breathe better. If you sit in a chair, make sure it is comfortable, preferably with a firm back, and not one in which you will fall asleep. If you can sit without support for your back, then sit on the edge of the chair. A small cushion under the feet can also help raise the knees and straighten the spine. If you prefer to sit on the floor, the use of either a meditation stool or one, two or three firm cushions is recommended to bring your hips higher than your knees. This will help you to keep the spine straight, and stop your legs from becoming numb (see illustrations on page 28). There are many different meditation cushions available, suitable for various sitting postures. Never sit completely back on them. A padded mat on which to rest the knees, feet and legs is also recommended.

Once in your chosen sitting position, gently sway your body slightly from side to side and from front to back. Try to find your centre of balance. With practise you should be able to judge this. If you are unsure, place your hands, palms up, underneath your posterior and become aware of your pelvic bones pressing against your hands. When

There are various postures for meditation, but beginners may find one of the above three the most comfortable: (A) Kneeling with one, two or three firm cushions. (B) Sitting on a firm chair with a straight back, and with a cushion under the feet. (C) Cross-legged with one, two or three firm cushions.

you move too far forward, they will feel sharp, and when you move too far back, they will disappear. When you feel the pelvic bones pressing against your hands without feeling too sharp, you should have found your centre of balance.

It should be noted that people who are thin in build may find the above exercise painful, and will find the pelvic bones sharp in their hands no matter what position they are in. The important aspect to remember is to keep the spine erect.

You may wish to use a cushion on your lap to rest your hands upon to stop your arms pulling on your shoulders; or cushions under the knees, if sitting cross-legged, to give you more support and avoid strain on the knees. At this stage it is up to you how you position your hands. Many prefer to leave them palms up, resting on the legs, near to the body, either cupped one over the other or separate from one another. There are various different hand mudras that can be used in meditation.

Your head should be at a level where your gaze naturally falls to the floor, approximately one metre in front of you. Let your jaw drop slightly, but keep the lips touching. This will help relax the facial muscles. Smile, then relax the smile, as this will also help relax the facial muscles. Keep your teeth slightly apart, with the tip of the tongue touching the front upper palate, just behind the front teeth. This helps to stop the flow of saliva and the need to swallow.

Try not to let your body slouch. Aim to keep your head balanced and your spine erect, and make sure that you feel comfortable. You will be in the same position for a while, and you do not want your body to start aching and distracting your attention. Some people find it helpful to imagine there is an invisible piece of string attached to the crown of their head, which is pulled up to straighten the head, neck and spine. Keeping the spine erect distributes the weight of the body evenly and reduces discomfort during meditation practice. It also helps to keep you more attentive and allows energy to flow more freely through the body. You may find it difficult at first because your back muscles are weak, but with practice they will become stronger. Any slight trembling felt in the back muscles should disappear as the body becomes accustomed to sitting upright.

If you find a part of the body starting to ache, it may be that your posture is not correct. Stop and adjust your sitting position and start again. If discomfort continues, seek expert advice about the way you sit.

Breathing and relaxing

It is beneficial to calm the mind and body before meditating and to check that you are breathing properly. The following exercises are useful for identifying and releasing any tension in the body, and identifying any shallowness in breathing. More relaxation exercises will be found elsewhere in this book.

1 Lie on your back (or sit in your preferred meditation position) with your eyes closed and become aware of your breathing. Breathe naturally for a few minutes, then mentally check for any tension in your body and begin to release it without strain or force. Start with your toes and feet, gradually working up to your head. Check that your fists are not clenched, your shoulders not hunched, etc. As you focus on each part, mentally say to yourself, 'My ... (name the part) is free from tension and totally relaxed'. Be aware of your breathing as you do this. With each out-breath feel that you are releasing tension.

If you have been lying on the floor, do not lean forward to get up as this can create tension in the neck and spine. Roll over on to your right side (or left if you find it more comfortable) and place your left hand (right hand if on your left side) on the floor, approximately one foot away from your chest. Then push yourself up by applying pressure to the floor with your hand.

2 This exercise can be practised in your preferred meditation position or lying on the floor. If lying on the floor, lie flat on your back, with your legs bent (knees drawn upwards), with your arms (palms of the hands facing upwards) along the side of your body. Concentrate upon your breath. Keep your breathing even. Check that you are filling the whole of your lungs with air. Your abdomen should rise and fall, and your chest expand and contract. You should be able to feel this happening. If it is difficult to detect, it may be that your breathing is shallow and that you are using only part of your lungs. Be aware of this and try to fill your lungs without straining or rushing – breathe a full, natural breath without force.

If you place one hand four fingers' breadth below your navel, you should be able to feel your abdomen rise and fall with each breath. You may be able to see your rib cage expand and contract. When you breathe in, try not to hold any tension in your body. Keep your abdomen relaxed. Let it slowly rise with the in-breath and sink down with the out-breath. It can be helpful to visualise the in-breath gently rising in a pyramid shape from your abdomen to your chest, or a 'v' shape from your navel, into your chest area (use whichever you find most helpful).

If you are unsure about your breathing, you may wish to seek advice from an experienced yoga practitioner. Most spiritual centres will have someone who can advise you on proper breathing.

3 In your preferred sitting position, become aware of your breathing. Exhale gently through your nostrils, and gently breathe in through them to the count of three. Hold your breath, without strain, to the count of three, then gently breathe out slowly to the count of three, emptying your lungs of air in a natural way without force, drawing in gently on the lower abdominal muscles at the end of each exhalation. Do this exercise five times. With each inhalation, breathe in all that is good and positive. With each exhalation, breathe out all that is negative. When you can comfortably breathe in and out, and retain your breath to the count of three, increase to the count of four, then five, but build up to this slowly over a period of time. This exercise energises the body and clears the mind, bringing both into a more responsive state for meditation practice.

If you have difficulty in holding your breath, practise without any breath retention until you are able to hold your breath comfortably without strain. Stop the practice if any discomfort is felt. We would like to warn against any drastic or prolonged changes to breathing unless under the direction of a knowledgeable meditation teacher, who can give guidance and explain the reasons for altering your breathing pattern. See also the following chapter on health problems and breath retention.

As you do this exercise, notice how your breathing changes your awareness. During the day, be aware of how your breathing affects you and how it changes depending on your state of mind. When you are calm, your breathing will be slow and even. When you are agitated, breathing becomes fast and and shallow. Through breath awareness we can calm the mind. This is why breath awareness is so important in the practice of meditation. If you are attentive to your breathing, you will discover an important and integral aid to spiritual awareness.

*   *   *

A personal realisation

My mind is immersed in the spiritual dimension of life. My actions are in line with spiritual living. I am an individual expression of God. I am perfect and complete. My life is rich in love and goodness, and open to infinite possibilities.

Fundamentals

Infinite Spirit, grant us Your wisdom,
so that we may grow in true knowledge
and understanding of Your ways.

There are various methods and practices of meditation. Some involve breath awareness, visualisation, or the repetition of a word or phrase. It is up to the individual to find a suitable practice. It is best to start with something simple, and not to chop and change too often. However, you may need to try several types of practice before you find one that is right for you. Remember that if meditation is a new activity in your life, it may take time to master and understand. Be prepared to give it a trial period of at least three months.

Problems with health

Any healthy-minded person should have no problem with meditation. But anyone diagnosed as psychotic, or who is extremely neurotic, would be best advised to seek professional help first, as meditation practice may cause withdrawal into a world of fantasy.

If you suffer from high blood pressure, a heart condition, severe asthma or any respiratory problems it is best to seek advice from both your doctor and an experienced meditation tutor before practising, especially before doing any exercise that may involve retention of the breath. Certain yogic breathing exercises have been found to be beneficial in these conditions, but it is essential to check first.

If any breathing practices cause you problems, meditation can still be practised as long as your mind and body are relaxed, your breathing rhythmic, and your mind focused upon the exercise.

If you suffer from nerves, find that sudden sounds affect you or have a heart condition, do make extra sure that you will not be interrupted. Safeguard against any disturbance in your meditation period.

Meditation experiences

If you experience something out of the ordinary, do not be frightened as you may just be feeling something that you are simply not used to. If it keeps happening and you are not sure that what you are experiencing is correct, consult a reputable and recommended meditation tutor before continuing.

Many people experience such sensations as expanding or floating. This is natural, and may be due to the mind, body and emotions adapting themselves to a new activity. Sensations such as tingling on the face could be due to becoming more aware of the skin's surface. They show how little aware we usually are of our bodily sensations.

Do not try to repeat any of these experiences. Instead allow your meditation practice to progress and be a receptive and active process. Try not to become attached to any experiences, or presuppose anything will happen. Trust your practice and allow it to peel away the outer layers of your personality.

Meditation in action

When you are practising, let your breathing find its own natural rhythm (even if you are using a breathing exercise). This should bring about steadiness. Fix your mind upon your meditation. Let go of all concern for the outside world. Do not try to force yourself to concentrate. If your mind wanders, simply acknowledge this and bring your attention back to your practice.

Meditation is not about making the mind empty, which is impossible to do. Nor should it be a process of numbing the consciousness, but of strengthening and developing awareness of one's mental processes in order to focus one's attention and quieten the mind. At first, you might find it difficult to hold your attention upon what you are doing for more than a few minutes. But gradually, with practice, you will find that you will be able to focus your attention for a longer period.

In the preliminary stages, all kinds of thoughts may start rising to the surface. This happens because you have stopped to look at what is going on inside yourself. An analogy is often drawn, comparing the mind to a pond that has been stirred up. We often stir up our minds by feeding in all kinds of thoughts and emotions, but with the help of meditation practice we have the opportunity to transform troublesome areas, settle our minds and become more peaceful. Through this we are able to still the surface of our minds and look more deeply into our nature and discover the true Self.

Watching the mind in meditation and everyday life

When practising meditation, you may find that your mind seems to become more active rather than restful. Old anxieties and experiences may start to surface. Emotions can rise up, the body become fidgety and noises distract you.

Observe these if they occur, but do not become involved in them or try pushing them away. Simply observe what is happening. (See Appendix 1 for further guidance on concentration.) One way to loosen the grip of such distractions is to identify and name them as they occur, for example 'body sensation', 'hearing sensation', 'feeling sensation', 'mind sensation'. But if a strong emotion does arise whilst meditating, you may need to look at it and discover what it is about before being able to 'dis-identify' from it. Meditation gives you the opportunity to do this. In some cases counselling may be helpful.

Watching the mind is a practice that can be done in everyday life. The following is a personal experience of a friend:

> I remember waiting outside a railway station when an unstable individual tried to cause trouble just when some friends had turned up to be taken to see an Indian holy man I knew. I instantly saw several options, such as being justly annoyed, retaliating, or playing the whole situation down so that it did not spoil my friends' evening out. I chose the latter and did my best to let it go. It was as though my mind had become a multi-CD player with a choice of which music to play.

The point about this observation is that there is a 'watcher' behind the roles we play. This watcher has the capacity to choose how situations affect us, and how we react to them. By strengthening awareness of this ability to stand back, observe and be attentive to what is going on in and around us, we become more knowledgeable of how we work psychologically and conscious of who we really are.

As you go through your day, see if you can be aware of the choices you have in activities you undertake. Be aware of the many different roles that you play in your life. See if you can be more conscious of the 'internal watcher'. This is not easy to do as we often get too caught up in our roles. Try to be aware that they are only things we do, and not what we are.

Time and length of meditation

There is no set time or length to practise meditation. To begin with you may find 10 to 15 minutes sufficient. Many people prefer to practise early in the morning and at sunset, or before retiring at night. You may find it best not to practise too late as the mind may be too tired to concentrate. What is important is the quality of your meditation, not its length or when you practise it. As you become more adept, you may find a longer period beneficial. A suitable length might be around 30 minutes, once or twice a day. If you have put aside a set time, there is less chance that it will be forgotten or missed because of other commitments. But even practising occasionally is better than not at all.

The reward of commitment

In the beginning you might be eager to practise meditating. It may be a new experience for you, bringing some instant benefit. But the mind soon becomes tired of routine and the pull of the outside world can often weaken your commitment. This is when you will have to show conviction in your practices, and to observe a certain amount of discipline. This may seem pointless to those who are restless and unprepared to make a full commitment. But reward will await those who make the effort. For those who make even the smallest steps towards the discovery of the true Self will taste the joyful experience of finding peace within.

When you first begin to meditate, you may on occasion feel that you are doing well, and at others that you are getting nowhere. Do not be quick to judge what you consider to be good or bad meditation. Continue with your practice. Do not think for a moment that any time you devote to mastering meditation is wasted. Remember that meditation cannot be measured by any experience other than how it changes our experience of life and how we respond to it.

* * *

Breath awareness meditation

1 Sit in your preferred meditation position with your eyes closed, keeping your spine erect. Mentally check that your body is steady.

2 Bring your awareness to your breathing, and watch the in- and out-breaths for one to two minutes.

3 As you breathe in, mentally say to yourself, 'I am breathing in'. As you breathe out, mentally say to yourself, 'I am breathing out'. Practise this for one to two minutes.

4 Keep your awareness on your breathing. As you breathe in, mentally say to yourself, 'I, a spirit, am breathing in'. As you breathe out, mentally say to yourself, 'I, a spirit, am breathing out'. Practise this for one to two minutes.

5 Let go of your awareness of your breathing for a minute and be still. Then return your awareness to the rhythm of your breathing. As you breathe in, mentally say to yourself, 'I breathe in spiritual energy'. As you breathe out, mentally say to yourself, 'I breathe out spiritual energy'. Practise this for one to two minutes.

6 Keep your awareness on your breathing. As you breathe in, mentally say to yourself, 'I am at one with God', and as you breathe out, 'I am at one with all beings'. Practise this for one to two minutes.

7 Let go of your awareness of your breathing and sit in the stillness, breathing gently and naturally. Let the stillness and silence pervade your whole being.

8 When you feel ready, become aware of your body and your environment with a sense of well-being.

Being

Make my mind tranquil and at peace
so I may reflect Your love more purely.

Meditation practice should become a natural and enjoyable part of our lives, and its influence reflected in the way we live. The following guidelines are given to help achieve success in this art:

1. Conduct and ethics

To obtain peace, balance and an inner and outer harmony in our life, it is necessary to live decently and with a sense of order. We should realise that we are citizens of the world and need to obey the laws of the world as well as the laws of God. We must strive to maintain good relationships with our family, friends and working colleagues. We must also strive to find our right place in the scheme of things so that we find a way to contribute to life and discover inner fulfilment.

2. Living by spiritual laws

We must try in our development to understand the implications of the law of cause and effect: as a man thinks and acts, so he becomes. We should understand how this leads us to express the law of association. We need to examine this law in our life – how we think, how our thought connects us with various levels of experience – and see if this is helping us to awaken to our spiritual consciousness. Is this helping us to associate with God and nature? Is this helping us to realise that we are one with all life?

3. Synchronising our thoughts, feelings and actions

Our state of consciousness is the result of what we continually think, feel and do. If we are to strive for the highest within us, we should attempt to have more control over our thoughts, feelings and actions by every means at our disposal, such as meditation, inspirational reading and associating with people who are constructive in their outlook. All these will help us to achieve this. We should not gossip or speak in a negative way. We must learn to synchronise our thoughts, feelings and actions so that they are in harmony with one another.

4. The process of spiritual attentiveness

To enter truly the silence and meditate properly, it is necessary to collect together our scattered thoughts. We must not allow our minds to be obstructed by physical matters or problems. We need to bring our minds to a one-pointed flow of attention so that we change the flow from worldly matters and direct it within. One way of doing this is to bring your mind to a state of knowing God within you, with the attention fixed at the point between your eyebrows. This is appropriate for 'thinking types'. For those who are 'feeling types', the attention can be fixed within the heart centre (middle of the chest), and the presence of God felt there. Just let your body relax. With your attention fixed at either of these two areas, you will find that your mental activity will settle down of its own accord.

If you have difficulty thinking and feeling with attention, a good exercise to begin with is breath awareness. Watch your breath as it flows in and out. Make no effort to control your breath, but just observe it flowing in and out. You will soon feel yourself becoming calmer and more objective. Thoughts will still float into your mind, but you will find that you pay less attention to them, and your thoughts will settle down. Practise watching your breath in this way until you feel that you are ready to centre your attention on the heart or eyebrow centres.

5. Being attentive within

The more practised you are at turning within, the more you will be able to focus your attention on meditation, and the more positive and smooth your unfoldment will be, outwardly as well as inwardly. It will help you to become a more effective person, spiritually and physically, in your life. It will also help you not only to quicken your spiritual unfoldment, but to accomplish much more in life. You will find yourself more decisive about your motives – spiritually and physically. You will find yourself more focused, less out-of-sorts.

You will learn how to live both inwardly and outwardly, and success in these areas will follow. You will notice less and less failure in your life. You will start to become a person of purpose and insight who knows no limitation. You will then bring your spirit's true purpose into activity.

6. The secret of concentration

In all activities of life, but more importantly in our spiritual life (particularly in meditation), we have to concentrate in order to perform any task well. When you sit quietly and become aware of God within, and as this awareness becomes stronger, try to focus your thoughts upon the fact that your real Self lives, moves and has its being in God. Centre your awareness upon this fact until it completely absorbs you.

In time you may become aware of an inner light, or a sense of joy and peace – an almost blissful feeling – or a greater sense of oneness with life. This will indicate that you are concentrating in the right manner. Whatever happens, give yourself to it, yield yourself to it, surrender your all to it, this is the secret.

To concentrate in this manner does not just mean thinking about it, or applying force to your thoughts. It is about letting the attention flow towards that sense of the thing – to let yourself merge and become one with it. Real meditation is not yearning to receive, but allowing the attention to flow towards God with a sense of aspiration. When you finish your meditation, you should always feel more at peace, happier and brighter. This will lead you to a state of oneness and joy in life.

7. A sense of oneness with all things

As your meditation deepens, you will find nature and life becoming more alive. Your life will take on a whole new meaning. Your relationships with people will acquire greater depth. Your ability to love will expand – you will find yourself becoming one with God. You will begin to realise that God is expressing Itself through you, as you, and is expressing Itself through everything and everyone. Try to remain aware of these feelings at all times.

You should find that after your practice of meditation, natural intuition will begin to function better. It will help and guide you. You will find your consciousness becoming more open, aware and impartial.

*   *   *

A personal realisation

I live, move and have my being in the stillness of God. The light of the Supreme Spirit shines through the whole of my being. My mind is quiet and receptive to the still, small voice within. I am tranquil, calm and at peace with all my thoughts, and with all that surrounds me.

Silence

*I give myself to God so I may be used
in whatever way God chooses to express.*

There are four important areas of spiritual unfoldment: the use of words, the power of thought, contemplation and silence. These may overlap and affect different areas of our development. All can be used in different types of practice – in prayer, meditation, mediumship, and even in our daily life. They should become part of our natural life, and their power should enhance our spiritual potential. But for any practice to be of value, we must be on our guard against dry routine and conscious of what we are doing.

Transformation through contemplation

Contemplation is about introspection and reflection. It is sometimes called the 'Prayer of the quiet mind'. But in fact it is the stepping stone that leads towards that goal, whether in prayer or meditation. However, terminology can differ. Contemplative prayer in Christian traditions has comparisons with silent meditation practices in Eastern traditions.

Contemplation helps us change our habitual flow of thinking from self-centredness to God-centredness. It focuses the conscious mind and develops our intuition so that our consciousness transcends worldly perception to more refined states of awareness. It helps us withdraw from restrictive patterns of thought and awaken to the Divine in all. Contemplation is the birth of spiritual attentiveness, and is linked with the development of the quiet mind. It is through contemplation that we learn how to quieten our worldly thoughts and become centred in God's presence.

If we look for the glory of God within ourselves, and in the world that surrounds us, we cannot behold anything without recognising its

43

cause – the spiritual activity behind the outward appearance. As we stand in awe of this Reality, we will find fewer extraneous thoughts arising in our minds. The more we are able to do this, the more we will be able to realise God's presence in all.

Contemplative practice

It is initially through the analytical part of the mind that we start to open ourselves to God, by examining our thoughts and our feelings, and identifying anything that creates the appearance of separation from God. We can then overcome any barriers that we may have created around our hearts, and allow our intuitive nature to function and blend more freely with the spiritual dimension of life. Modern psychology has noticed two distinct functions of the brain. The left hemisphere is associated with analytical, logical, linear and intellectual thought while the right hemisphere is linked to perceptual, organisational, creative and intuitive thought.

In order to develop spiritually, we have to examine ourselves, our lives and our beliefs. We need to find time to reflect and search our innermost selves. Remember, you are the only person on this earth who can truly know *you*. Discover who you are and how you feel about life. Face up to yourself and recognise the creative force of life working through you. If you have the vision to see beyond the surface and look for the Divine in all, you will discover a peace and oneness that pervades all life.

Through the process of knowing ourselves we become aware of what is happening at various levels of our being. We also become aware of what may need to be looked at, changed, or overcome. We discover all the potential good that is within us, and find ways of bringing it to the surface and having more influence on our lives.

Contemplation helps us to free our minds from past associations, and to realise that there is more to life than just our bodies, minds and emotions. It helps us to connect more with others and life around us.

Take time to look for and experience God's Presence within you and within the world around you. Look for it in the setting of a golden sun, in the sound of a running stream, or in the rustling of leaves in the wind. Reflect upon all things and draw positive strength from them. Let all these things awaken the God-spirit within. Let contemplation lift your consciousness in order to create an atmosphere of quiet receptivity where God and the spirit can be perceived.

It is at this point that contemplation overlaps into the next stage of awareness: silence.

The master key of silence

Silence, whether in meditation, prayer or mediumistic development, is the most important ingredient for successful practice. It is in periods of silence that God and the spirit can influence us at deeper and more profound levels. It is here that our spiritual potential is refined.

We should not be alarmed at the idea of silence, but let its mystery lead us towards finding peace within – a peace that becomes the very heart of our life, enriching our souls and leading us to a greater awareness of all things. For it is not through intellectual reasoning that God and the spirit are eventually found or through our physical senses. They are reached through the intuitive mind penetrating and influencing our thoughts and feelings, and awakening us to a greater level of being. God and the spirit are eventually found by slowing down all worldly thoughts and placing ourselves in a silent and receptive state of awareness.

You may wonder, 'If what we are seeking is beyond intellectual understanding, does this imply that we are wasting the time we spend on books, prayers or discussions concerning God and the spirit?'. It does not, because anything that can help us reach that point of attunement is of value. Time given to reflection, widening and focusing our consciousness will lead us to a personal awakening. All these activities can serve as springboards into the depths of direct experience. Until we have reached that stage, we will need as much help and encouragement as we can get.

The still, small voice within

Let that inner stillness open you, so that you discover that sacred place within. Once achieved, you can rest, recollect and revitalise the whole of your being and discover 'the still, small voice within'. In discovering this stillness, you will find that level whereby God and the spirit may influence and work through you, and lead you to richer levels of being and consciousness.

Do not be afraid of this silence, but welcome it as a friend and companion on your spiritual journey – share with it your very Self. Let it help you to help God and the spirit awaken within you – as indeed it will – the limitless potential which is yours. Let silence take you to that higher consciousness. Let the silence within you *be*. Let the God within you *be*. Let the spirit working through you *be*, that this experience will help you understand the *real* you, as you really are!

*   *   *

A day working on yourself

Make time to be silent and quieten your mind, body and emotions. If at all possible, spend a whole day in total silence. Be aware of the peace and silence. Let it permeate your whole being and all things around you. Do not concern yourself with troubles of the outside world. Spend your day in prayer, reflection and meditation. Read a short passage from a spiritual book. Reflect upon the inner Self. Walk in the open air, and reflect upon the Spirit in all life. Let these activities encourage and help you to quieten your mind.

Sit quietly and ask yourself questions such as: 'Who am I?'; 'What direction is my life taking?'; 'Is there anything stopping me from unfolding my spiritual nature?'. See what this reveals and let it change your perceptions about yourself and your life.

Rest for a while in the Spirit's presence. Select a word or short sentence that expresses your intention of opening and giving yourself over to the Spirit. Say it once in your mind, then be silent and reflect upon it. If anything disturbs you in this time, repeat the word or sentence and go back to being still and silent again, but do not have expectations about what may or may not happen.

As you do this exercise, try to remain open and aware of anything that you may experience. If you feel moved to express your feelings by painting, writing or by sending out distant healing thoughts, then do so. Let the influence and inspiration of the inner Self come through into your daily life and activities.

You will find that days spent alone in silence will be of more value to you than you may realise. It is through such periods of inner silence and reflection that we strengthen our link with God and the spirit.

Exercises

Help me to rise above my mind, body and emotions,
and to realise that I am much more than these things.

The following meditations will help to foster awareness and sensitivity. They will help you to become conscious of how your thought affects your development. This is important because it is through thought that God and the spirit communicate.

We must understand that thought vibrates, has motion, volition and the power to act independently, and that the ultimate independent power acting in the universe is Spirit. We need to prepare our conscious self so that these thoughts, and the accompanying vibrations and changes of energy, can take root in our unconscious and become a permanent fixture in our conscious minds. Each time we turn our conscious thoughts to these meditations, our unconscious minds will know at once what is being done. Through it the creative process will come into play.

This is why it is important to understand the role of thought and feeling in development. It is why meditation works as it changes our perspective. Without this change, it would be difficult to co-operate with God or the spirit, and to offer what they need.

These meditations will help you understand and work with the spirit that you are. For if we are going to work with God or the spirit, we must lose all sense of limitation and realise that the same Spirit is in all. Through this we will develop a sense of openness to all possibilities. We should never deny or suppress any aspect of ourselves as it is by facing up to the whole of what we are that we become more self-aware.

Awareness meditation 1[2]

This meditation helps to withdraw the conscious mind from outer activity and focus it on one's inner spirit nature. It will help you to become aware of qualities that affect all levels of yourself and affirm the finer aspects. You may wish to use only one or two of the qualities in step 5 and meditate on them for longer.

1 Sit in an upright but relaxed position. Let all tension go. Allow your mind to become absorbed in your breathing. Watch your in- and out-breaths for about three minutes. Do not strain.

2 With each inhalation, feel your body and mind relax. Feel yourself to be alive and well. With each exhalation, imagine that all negatives, past and present, are leaving you. Practise for about three minutes.

3 Continue to concentrate on your breathing and mentally repeat, 'I am at peace'. Have a sense of being filled with peace, free from all tension and bondage. Repeat three times.

4 Pause for approximately one minute and breathe freely, feeling detached from all things.

5 Begin again, concentrating on your breathing and repeat the following phrases on the in- and out-breaths: in-breath, 'Love is my true nature'; out-breath, 'Not anger'. In-breath, 'Openness is my true nature'; out-breath, 'Not limitation'. In-breath, 'Acceptance is my true nature'; out-breath, 'Not denial'. In-breath, 'Compassion is my true nature'; out-breath, 'Not hatred'. In-breath, 'Freedom is my true nature'; out-breath, 'Not restriction'.

Repeat each pair of statements three times. After each pair, take a minute to absorb its meaning.

Awareness meditation 2

1   Breathe in and feel within your breathing a sense of being at one with God. Repeat either of the following two affirmations:

God's power works through me, as me.
God's power, love and light fills my very being.

Try to be aware of God's power within your whole being. Be positive and know the statement to be true. As you breathe out, try to be aware that you are one with God, that you are an instrument through whom God's power is pouring itself. Pray that God will help you to accomplish all that you must. Stay with this practice for approximately ten minutes.

2   Breathe in, and feel and know that you are one with God and the spirit – one with your own spirit and the spirit world. As you breathe out, seek the spirit's aid to help you develop and to keep an open mind. Do this for approximately five to ten minutes.

3   As you breathe in, breathe in a sense of God. As you breathe out, imagine that you are filling your aura with this thought. Feel that your aura is expanding and that you are now linked to, and have a greater sense of oneness with, the whole of life. Continue for approximately five minutes.

4   Finish by becoming aware of your body and the room in which you are sitting, then gently stretch.

PART TWO

Attunement

Proceed gently, sensibly and wisely.

Psychic Awareness

I behold the Invisible in the visible.
I recognise Its power manifesting through all.

People have understood and used psychic powers since ancient times. Their use can be found in nearly all religious traditions. The third part of Patanjali's *Yoga Aphorisms*, which dates back to around the second century CE, deals with the development of the *siddhis* (psychic powers). Like the superknowledges in Buddhism, these powers are aspired to in order to help the yogin overcome the effects of karma and attain freedom.[3]

Much has been written about psychic and mediumistic phenomena. Some people believe that psychic and mediumistic abilities are detrimental to spiritual life. But this is only true if they are developed at the expense of spiritual awareness.

Others believe that mediumship is a spiritual gift, separate from the psychic aspect of our nature. Many teachers of mediumship regard it as being higher than the psychic. Yet if we look closely, it is plain that it is in fact a psychic power and not necessarily a spiritual one.

Mediumship works through the same internal mechanisms of perception that are used to perceive the physical world. We would know nothing of the world if it was not for our psychic senses: everything we perceive is processed through them. We experience everything in symbolic form, which has symbolic meaning to us, including language and all other sensory data. We can know nothing of life until it is first perceived as a psychic image.

Psychic and spiritual awareness

Mediumship by itself does not require us to develop qualities of spirituality, such as compassion, kindness, wisdom, discernment, and other attributes of a spiritual life and consciousness.

To become in tune with the spiritual dimension of life will require personal effort. There are exceptions where spirit intervention during a peak or mystical experience has changed a person's attitude and outlook on life. But this kind of experience may happen just once in someone's life. Personal effort and responsibility are still required.

We should have practical understanding about the difference between the psychic and the spiritual. Throughout human history, there have been instances of people having mediumistic experiences which did not change them spiritually in any way.

Mediumship is an ability much like any other. It operates through the mind. Its results are coloured by the character and personality of the individual. Some mediums have developed their mediumistic powers to a high degree, but not displayed any change in their personal and spiritual nature. From this we can deduce that we are dealing with a psychic, not a spiritual, phenomenon.

We must remember that the majority of spirit communicators have only recently passed to the spirit world. They may not have spiritually progressed any more than when they were alive on this earth. Having the ability to be aware of them does not make us spiritual.

The dictionary defines a psychic as being someone who is sensitive to forces or influences not recognised by physical laws. The word 'psychic' encompasses the soul, the spirit, the inner man or woman and the mind. Psychic abilities are about awareness of certain non-physical influences. People who have mediumistic experiences describe how they get an impression or flash of something, a sense of seeing or feeling someone. This occurs through the psyche and the unconscious and conscious mind.

These all relate to our inner being, to who and what we are. Because they relate to our inner self, we have to ask ourselves: 'Are we spiritually aware?'; 'Do we practise spiritual disciplines?'. Although a discarnate spirit can communicate through an individual's psychic or mediumistic powers, we must ask ourselves whether the communicator is spiritually aware.

These points are made not to discredit the views of others, but to emphasise that our spiritual growth is in our own hands, and is not the responsibility of any exterior influence. Even though any effort we are prepared to make spiritually will attract corresponding influences that will enhance our development, it is still up to us to make the effort.

Working at the level of our understanding

Sometimes we can see mediumship working at a person's individual level of understanding. For instance, at a public demonstration a medium gave messages which, although accepted as reasonably good evidence by everyone he went to, were all to do with material things, such as a pint of beer, a bottle of Scotch, or a plate of prawn sandwiches! Some mediums give messages that are always centred around someone's clothing or jewellery, but give little evidence of a person's inner nature and character. This kind of evidence can be useful, but if mediums constantly work at this level, and none other, it shows they have not developed or taken a wide enough view of mediumship.

Levels of awareness

There is much that we do not understand about the human mind and consciousness. There is more that we do not understand about our spiritual nature. In the past we may have been influenced in our thinking about these matters by the beliefs of others. Now we must take the opportunity to discover for ourselves their truth or falsehood.

There is danger in trying to distinguish between the prophet and the seer, the psychic and the mediumistic, the inspirational and the intuitive. All have their source in our being and their origin and expression in our souls, spirits and minds. All are but a flowing towards a discovery of the infinite potential within us.

These powers which manifest in our development are simply a means by which we can demonstrate that there is something beyond the physical. But ask yourself: 'What is it? Psychic, mediumistic or spiritual?'. Beliefs will differ about what these things may or may not be. But beliefs can conflict and confuse, whereas provable facts do not. So search, and discover the truth for yourself: this is all part of what spiritual growth is about.

The ultimate goal

If approached correctly, psychic and mediumistic development should lead us to understand the whole of our being, and bring us in tune with all life around us. Development should be grounded in a dedication to awakening to our spiritual consciousness. Although it is already within us, we still have to awaken to it. If we are to be representatives of the Supreme Spirit – either as mediums or advocates for the spiritual life – our lives should be a reflection of that Reality.

Psychic and mediumistic abilities by themselves do not necessarily indicate spiritual growth. They are no different from any other ability: they are neither good nor bad. It is what we do with these abilities that determines their worth. If we learn how to use them wisely and selflessly, they may become something of real value.

Psychic and mediumistic abilities are neither unnatural nor supernatural as they are a product of natural and intrinsic laws in all human life. Those people who have had a premonition, or followed up something as simple as a hunch, will have discovered this for themselves. To deny these faculties exist can mean ignoring an inherent and integral part of our nature which is as vital as any of our other senses. We would hardly wish to stop them from working.

Many have been born with psychic and mediumistic abilities; many have found these abilities *naturally* unfolding through a variety of spiritual practices. Masters of Yoga tell us that through practising yogic postures and breath awareness, psychic and clairvoyant abilities can develop, even if one is not actively trying to do so.

But whatever use these abilities may have, the purpose in developing them should be to help us be receptive to our 'true nature' and to expand our spiritual awareness. They should lead and open us to a much wider vision, which expresses itself in every area of our lives. The emphasis should be on personal development. This way, the problem of any ability becoming a distraction to spiritual growth will be less likely.

*   *   *

Visualisation exercise

The following exercise is useful for developing one's power of concentration and visualisation, and for stimulating the psychic senses from a visual and sensing point of view:

1   Ask a friend to sit quietly for you as a subject for this exercise. Visualise that you are together in a garden or meadow. Look about you

to see what flowers there are. In the garden there are cultivated flowers of all types whilst the meadow has a variety of wild flowers. Take time to observe the flowers. Get a sense and feel of them.

2   While keeping in mind the friend you are sitting with, allow your senses to be drawn to one type of flower that represents his or her character and personality. Describe the flower, its colour, its variety and say why it represents these to you psychically.

3   Now move on to another type of flower which you feel links with your friend's emotions and feelings. Say why this particular flower is indicative of these.

4   Let your awareness be drawn to another type of flower which relates to your friend's potential. Say why the image and colour of the flower gives you this information.

5   Now move on to another flower that draws your psychic senses towards it, one which relates to your friend's spiritual aspirations. Once again, describe the information you pick up from this flower, and why.

6   Still in the garden or meadow, move away from your friend and towards the spirit world that links with him or her. Become aware of a spirit presence that draws you towards another variety of flower. Ask yourself why this flower is being shown to you. How does it relate to that spirit presence? What message does it convey to your friend?

7   Blend with the spirit presence and become aware of who they are, and what they are trying to convey to you. Ask why this entity is communicating.

8   When you feel that this communication is ceasing, sit quietly with your friend in the garden or meadow and start to perceive how nature and colour speak to you.

Note: Those who are artistically inclined may wish to look for symbols and describe how they convey information to you. You might want to try this exercise by visualising yourself and a friend in a room, standing before an easel with a canvas and some paints. You then visualise painting shapes or a scene which depict the main elements of the exercise, and explain what they mean.

Those who are musically inclined may wish to find musical scales, chords, songs or hymns which depict the main elements of the exercise.

These visualisations are tools to give the mind something on which to concentrate and train its powers of attention on. In time you will let go of these props and allow the flow of the psychic self to function naturally.

The Aura

*Widen my awareness, so I may develop
and receive more of Your gracious light.*

The aura is constructed of many levels or different grades of vibrations. In literature about the aura, and in accounts of those who claim to perceive it, we often find contradictions about what the aura is and of what it consists. It all comes down to investigation, perception and psychic awareness.

We are constantly learning more about the human personality. It may well be that there are levels beyond what we can perceive or understand, so any hard and fast approach to this subject could prove to be limiting. The following is merely a brief description and a personal view of *some* levels of our being, which relate to various levels found within the human aura. By understanding these, we not only come to know and understand ourselves, but also come to realise the various forces at work in all human life.

The spirit

The highest principle in man or woman is the spirit, and it is this which gives life to our physical form. It is the eternal 'I', the God within, the part that links us with the creative principle in all life. It is the true Self, the eternal good, which is constantly trying to tell us how we should be, and seeks to provide us with limitless potential at every level of our being. We must therefore try in our development to understand this higher Self and observe how it functions through us, and why. We must endeavour to awaken to the spirit within as well as the Spirit in all life. By doing so, we will open ourselves to a variety of possibilities and experience.

Some people believe there is a separate level for the soul while others maintain that the soul is another term for the 'God-spirit within', what the Hindu tradition terms the *Atman*. Some call this separate level the 'causal body', which is said to be the product of all that is good in life, made up of the mental level's highest attributes.

The soul is seen as the Spirit individualised, the higher consciousness in human beings, a vehicle through which the Supreme Spirit can express Itself. It is through it that we come to realise the God in all.

Whether this separate level serves another purpose to intuition or is different from, or the same as, the God-spirit within, we leave the reader to decide.

The intuitive and the inspirational

There is something in each of us which knows itself to be more than the body. We can term this state of knowing as being a high form of intuition. Its development can be likened to an echo of the spirit, something within our consciousness that keeps endeavouring to bring to the surface of our mind a superior sense of being. When this level is highly developed, we experience the reality behind the appearances of the world. We discover unity in all life, and through that unity inspiration flows as a creative force.

Intuition is an activity of the right side of the brain which draws mainly on unconscious material. It can function on a spiritual, mental or emotional level. Certain individuals experience intuition in the form of physical sensations, such as tingling of the skin, or notice a tightening in the stomach – what some people call a 'gut feeling'.

Intuition is often more developed in those who have a high degree of imagination, such as children and artists. Women are generally more intuitive than men. It is an essential part of psychic and mediumistic awareness. On an everyday level, it functions in the form of hunches and feelings of 'knowing' when one is on the right track.

The mental level: the will and the intellect

Both the will and the intellect are important functions of the mind. The will is a product of the conscious mind and is something that can be used by it. Through the use of the will we can have control over conscious thought and behaviour. But the will cannot *directly* affect our unconscious instincts and behaviour, although it can have substantial indirect influence over them through conscious processes.[4]

The will is one of various mental activities which entail focusing our awareness in order to carry out specific tasks to satisfy certain needs. It is a vital ingredient in self-realisation and spiritual development, for it can be used to overcome inner conflict and negative character traits, as well as to direct and focus our attention in periods of meditation.

The intellectual level is connected with activities of the left side of the brain, such as logical, rational and analytical thinking. Whilst our senses supply us with information, it is the intellect that tells us what it is we are sensing. There is some debate about 'nature versus nurture', as to whether 'intelligence' (a problem word for many to define and agree upon) is an innate product of the genes, or if it can be acquired and cultivated. The truth could well lie in a combination of the two.

Our intellect can be used for different types of thinking. On a simplistic level, we could perhaps talk of 'practical' and 'specialist' uses of the intellect. The first is about everyday life and understanding, and the latter is concerned with developed knowledge in a particular area. One might have specialist knowledge, but not be very effective on a practical, everyday level.

It is important to balance the intellect with the intuitive level so that one does not inhibit the other. Although inspiration functions through the intuitive level, one's intellect can help to give it more form and structure. For instance, a writer may have a flash of inspiration and write wildly for hours. But after this period, the writer will often need to analyse the content as well as edit and arrange it into more logical order and sentences. The ability to understand language and writing is also a 'left-brain' activity.

Emotions: possible links with instincts and cultural conditions

We all have natural instincts and emotions that work through our personality and character. It is through the mind and its connections with the senses that emotions are generated. Generally, we respond to sensory information by appraising things as potentially good or bad, after which emotions arise according to the judgement we have made.

Rarely, if ever, do we experience one emotion on its own. Some take the extreme view that the emotion of aggression is something that we all possess instinctively, and needs to be released. This can be done by channelling it into various activities, such as sport. Nonetheless, this does not fit with our experience of everyone we meet. A more accurate view seems to be that aggression can often be the result of environmental conditions and restraints. As human beings, we may feel the need to socialise and have different types of relationships in order to fulfil certain goals, desires and needs. When we receive more than we expect, it often makes us happy. But when these are not being met, it often causes frustration. This can surface in the form of aggression, or in other moods, such as depression or apathy.

We also possess various automatic responses that we share with other creatures on this earth, such as the 'fight or flight' response, and we are not the only life form that displays affection. Cultural differences can also have a large influence on the way we act. Different countries have different standards of behaviour which affect the way people emotionally express themselves.

On the whole, the emotional level of our being is about the way we act and respond to life, and has much to do with the psychological self, habitual self and worldly personality and character of each of us. However, heightened emotions of love, awe and ecstasy can have a transcendent function and, as a product of evolution and nature, a refined level of our instincts, like our higher Self, may also be trying to encourage each of us to develop and find our true place in the universe.

We should strive to become aware of the various conscious and unconscious forces working within and around us, how they affect and influence our lives and cultivate more positive qualities, such as compassion and openness. We also need to find ways of releasing any accumulated stress caused by modern living, and become more aware of our needs. Through this we will develop and discover more peace in life.

The physical level

Our bodies are made up of atoms that are the building blocks of all physical life. We should realise that nothing in nature is wasted. Our physical bodies are the product of atoms that once made stars, plants and other life in the universe.

It is within the physical body's aura that some mediums and psychics claim to be able to perceive disease and health problems, although some say that the latter are first detected in the energy body. Mediums often referred to this as the 'etheric body'. They tell us that every organ and cell has its own vibration and pattern of energy, which can be perceived within the auric field.

We should realise that our bodies exist because of their spiritual counterparts. The spirit seeks to work through our bodies, minds and feelings in order to express itself in and through all that we do. A combination and balance of the spirit, and the intuitive, mental, emotional and physical levels of our being will produce a balanced, well-rounded, holistic approach to life in us.

The energy body

Surrounding and working within everyone there exists a non-physical level of energy and activity. It is affected by all other levels of our being, including our conscious and unconscious minds. Various mediums believe this energy is used in the production of mental and physical mediumship as well as in healing. Objective clairvoyants say that it can be seen surrounding the physical body. Those who are sensitive to it say that it can be experienced constantly changing and working within and around the body. But what this energy is and what it does is by no means clear, and has not yet been recognised by modern science.

Some people call this level the 'subtle body', whilst others term it the 'etheric body'. There are various views about its function and use. People perceive and interpret this field of energy in different ways, and have varying ideas about the way it affects us as well as how we can affect it. The Chinese talk about the '*chi* energy' whereas yogis mention '*pranic* energy'. Whether these are terms for a similar thing, or for different levels of activity, is a matter for further investigation.

All levels of our being will vibrate as a variety of colours within the auric field. These colours all have quite specific meanings connected to different levels of our being. Nonetheless, all levels are interconnected and influence one another. Some say that there are certain colours that are static. If this is so, we must ask ourselves why, as we are constantly changing. Therefore, so must the colours within our aura. They may well represent potential that has not yet been realised.

On the whole, the colours within the aura constantly alter as one changes one's thoughts, feelings, environment, etc. As we grow in our development, certain changes will happen within us which will be reflected within our aura. To understand what the various colours in the aura mean we need to develop our intuitive, analytical and psychic senses, and understand them in relation to the person with whom we perceive the colours.

*   *   *

Sensing the aura

These exercises will increase your sensitivity to energies in the aura:

Exercise 1

To begin to sense the aura, place both hands together in an attitude of prayer. Draw the hands out to the level of your shoulders. Keep your eyes open and your awareness centred in the space between the palms. Slowly bring them nearer until you feel that you have an invisible balloon between your palms. This is the energy from your physical aura.

Exercise 2

Stand one pace back behind a friend, holding your hands up (palms facing forwards), and move slowly towards your friend until you can sense his or her aura, approximately two inches away from his or her shoulders. Try to sense the energy of your friend's aura in your hands. Ask your friend to recall different memories, such as those associated with love, fear or hate, or thoughts of someone they love who is living on this earth or in the spirit world. Ask your friend to think of healing and to imagine various colours. See if you can sense a change in the energies around him or her.

Suggestions for further exercises

(a) If you are an objective clairvoyant, look at people and see if you can begin to perceive a sort of misty outline around them. Keep this in clairvoyant view and see what may build from this. If you see colour, be aware that it emanates from the person. Try to understand what it tells you about him or her.

(b) Take a flower. Go beyond its physical shape with the mind and find out what you see, what you feel. Try to understand its energy.

(c) Hold an object that belongs to someone and use psychometry (the ability to feel an object psychically and pick up information relating to the person that it belongs to) to sense the aura and see what information comes from it.

Psychometry is a useful tool as it relates to the aura and enables you to understand a person's psychic activity. It is one of the most useful abilities a medium can develop.

Colour Awareness

The spirit within me houses only perfection.

To develop an understanding of the colours that can be perceived in the human aura, we need some knowledge of colour and how we view it, both physically and clairvoyantly.

Seeing colour

We perceive colour because of various wavelengths of light that are either absorbed or reflected by what we see. In 1802, an English physicist, Thomas Young, first put forward a theory suggesting that, just as all colours in the spectrum can be produced by mixing paints of only three primary colours – red, blue and yellow – so too could our eyes contain receptors which are sensitive to these three colours, and that all other colours we perceive are produced from different combinations of just these three receptors. In 1964, this idea, known as the Trichromacy Theory, was confirmed, but it was discovered that in humans the three receptors were in fact sensitive to red, green and purple.[5]

Every colour has its own wavelength. Red is said to be the longest. This then changes through the spectrum to violet, which is the shortest. Beyond this we move into ultra-violet rays and X-rays, which are beyond the normal human capacity of perception.

Any coloured object we perceive absorbs all other colours in the spectrum, except the colour which the object is perceived to be. That colour is reflected by the object, which we perceive through our optic nerves. Our brain then deciphers the colour's specific wavelength and gives us the impression of the colour. Pure colours of light that are made up of a single wavelength are rarely seen by our eyes. For instance, the red of a flower, though consisting mostly of red, may have within it a certain amount of blue and green, and will reflect these colours as well as the red. When all colours are absorbed, it will appear black. When equal amounts of all colours in the spectrum are reflected, white light is produced.

When we see colours clairvoyantly through our psychic senses, our brain, mind, instinctive and intuitive senses will perceive colour in very much the same manner as we do when seeing through our physical senses. The mind will decipher colour by using the same process of recognising colour wavelengths, as it does when seeing colours physically, except it does so without the use of the physical eyes, because we are not perceiving physical colours. Yet the same principles of colour seem to apply to the non-physical dimensions of life, as they do to the physical dimension. If this were not so, we would not be able to classify correctly any colours that we perceived through our psychic senses.

The variety of colour

Whether we approach the subject of colour from an artistic, scientific or clairvoyant point of view, there are no strict rules when it comes to the theory of colour. We should realise that within just one single hue of colour, there is a tremendous range. For example, to the the trained eye, it is possible to differentiate more than 50 varying shades of blue. If we then consider changing the tone of all these blues, by making them darker or lighter, we would discover within this single range of blue well over 100 colour variations. Adding yellow (which has approximately the same amount of variations) to the blue will produce an enormous variety of greens, and bluish and yellowish greens. If we next consider using the colour red, and also take into account the density or translucent quality of colour, the variations of all these colours will run to hundreds, if not thousands, of distinguishable hues and colour combinations.[6]

An artist's colour wheel

The spectrum is often divided into six or seven bands. The colour wheel on the right shows the various mixes of six colours found in the spectrum (indigo, the seventh, falls in between the blue and violet area). In artist's terms, we can produce these colours by mixing pigments of just the three primary colours – red, blue and yellow – creating a complete range of secondary colours.

Opposite each colour you will find its complementary colour – one which is made up of its exact opposite – so on the opposing side to red you will find green, which is made from yellow and blue. If an artist were to use these complementary colours together, they would create the maximum visual impact; whereas colours closely related to each other on the wheel would create more of a sense of colour harmony.[7]

But there is a difference between the way colours react and mix when using pigment as opposed to light. For example, if red and green paints were mixed together, they would create brown, but if red and green lights were overlapped they would make yellow. The three primary colours are also different (see diagram below).

Coloured light

The diagram shows spectrum colours, as formed by overlapping various proportions of primary coloured light – red, blue and green (called 'mixing by addition').[8]

Mixed in varying proportions, these three colours can produce almost any colour in the spectrum.

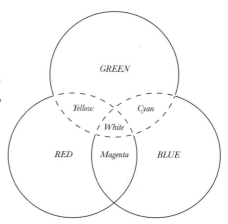

Mediumistic interpretation of colour

Though some colours may have an almost universal interpretation, we should realise that they will mean different things to different people, and will affect them differently. Obviously colours have emotional meanings, but these may vary from one person to another. Also, a colour may change its meaning and interpretation when seen alongside other colours.

When we perceive colour in someone's aura, we should try to feel into the colour, and link with that person without any preconceived ideas of what the colour may or may not represent. We should look at the saturation of the colour as well at its density or translucent quality. If you perceive colours clairvoyantly, you should remember the vast range of colours that there are. If you see blue, for example, ask yourself what shade you are perceiving. Are there hints of any other colours mixed with it? Is it a distinct, particular shade of blue? How dark or bright is it? What other colours are there around the colour? Only when you have done this should you seek to find out what the colour represents.

*   *   *

Developing an awareness of colour

The three simple awareness exercises that follow can help cultivate both an inner and outer awareness of colour. There is a danger of becoming too inward looking, so a balance between inner and outer awareness is important. These exercises can put us more in touch with ourselves and with life around us, and help develop our sensitivity. They are therefore helpful in both personal and mediumistic development.

Exercise 1: Inner awareness

1   Sit in a chair with your eyes closed and be still and quiet for a few moments.

2   Visualise yourself sitting in the middle of a room that is completely white. Imagine that everything in the room has been painted white: the floor, the ceiling, the windows and any furniture you see in the room.

3   Stay in this room for a few moments and ask yourself how it makes you feel. Do you feel cold, peaceful or uplifted? Or does this room make you feel agitated or indifferent? Whatever you feel, observe it and try to identify it.

4   Now try changing the colour of the room to another hue and see if you notice a difference in your feelings. Then try other colours and observe your responses.

5   Imagine that the room is completely green. Then visualise yourself in a forest, surrounded by different shades of green. Try to see these in your mind's eye. Feel into them and see how they affect you. See if you notice a difference between being in a green room and being in a green forest.

Exercise 2: Outer awareness

1   Find time to be alone in nature and near some trees. Sit down or slowly walk around in a quiet and peaceful frame of mind.

2   Observe how much variety of colour there is in nature. See how a single tree can have so many different shades of green in its leaves. If you do this exercise in autumn or winter, you will find a myriad of yellow-browns and reds in the colour of the leaves. Notice the play of light and shade on the trees and on the ground. Look at the texture and various colours in the bark of the trees. Observe the ground beneath your feet and how it is not just one shade. Note how the colours in one tree are different from those in another, and how different the colours of the trees are from any bushes or grass areas.

3   Now observe how you respond to the colours you are contemplating and see how they affect you. How do they make you feel?

This exercise can be done at any time, and anywhere. As you walk down the street in a busy city you can observe the play of light and colour on the buildings and shops and be aware of how much colour and light there is in a street. Be open to life around you, conscious of how you react to it.

Exercise 3: Stretching your awareness and sensitivity

1   Collect a variety of different coloured plain (not patterned) scarfs, ribbons or papers. Place them in front of you and pick out one colour and see if you get a feeling or impression from it. Look at it and feel into it. Analyse your impressions.

71

2   Choose another colour or shade and see if you discover any difference.

3   Now place the two colours together and see if that tells you anything more.

4   Add a third colour and see if that changes your impression in any way.

5   Ask yourself questions about these colours and shades. Do they make you feel happy or sad, heavy or light? What kind of energy or vibration do you get from them?

6   Put the colours back and choose three, four or five to which you feel drawn. Tell yourself that these colours are to represent various aspects of your own personality. See what you can discover about these colours and what they reveal about yourself. Make a note of what transpires during this experiment, as you may wish to refer back to it for direction later on or to see how things have changed if you do the exercise another time.

This exercise can be taken a stage further by asking a friend, and then someone you do not know so well, to choose some colours, and see what impressions you get from them. Ask them to be honest and tell you how accurate you were.

Mediumistic Development

May my eyes see with the spirit's vision.
May my ears hear the sound of a voice long-still.
May my senses feel the closeness of those much loved again.

Most mediumistic development groups sit in a circle. The reason for this is that it places the sitters equally apart and gives them their own psychic and spiritual space. The circle is a symbol of wholeness and unity.

The motive of the circle and of the sitters should be for each sitter to develop psychic power or energy over a period of time. This will enable those in the spirit world to make their presence known to members of the group, and supply them with an on-going process for development.

If the motive is right, spirit personalities will bring their own energy and power to blend with the circle. It is through that blending that the sitters will in time come to know who is mediumistic. It will then become the responsibility of the other sitters to encourage the potential medium to develop trust and become responsive to the influences working with them.

This is, of course, a very basic description of sitting in a development group. We do not wish to presume how the spirit world would wish your circle to develop. This is part of the discovery of the group, and we would not want to interfere with that on-going process.

Rules and regulations, such as how and how not to run a circle, can be restrictive, not just from the sitters' point of view, but more importantly from the spirits'. We suggest that you read the following points very carefully. Remember there is no substitute for sound common sense and rational judgement.

Elements to apply to successful psychic and mediumistic development

1. Sitters

The sitters must be sincere, well-balanced people whose minds are open, and hopefully of a spiritual temperament, whose main aim is to build a link of communication with the spirit world. The purpose of any circle, and of those who sit in it, is to develop to the point at which they open to the spirit's influence, and through that discover various truths about the spirit. There must be the clear desire to move from the physical to the spiritual level of perception.

2. Time and place

Sitting at a regular time and place is important because it brings discipline into your life and into the development of the circle. As time goes on and somebody shows signs of mediumship, you will realise that this self-discipline has helped establish the right atmosphere and vibration. This will enable you eventually to unfold the many different levels of mediumship.

3. Potential

Sitters may or may not show signs of mediumistic potential. If you are unsure about your abilities, do not be deterred from sitting and exploring possibilities of mediumistic potential.

4. Attitude

Reverence and the desire to be of use to the spirit world are essential, as is a willingness to dedicate time to explore and understand the spirit, and the implications of its influence on you and those around you.

5. Co-operation

All sitters will have to learn how to co-operate with each other and with the spirit world as well as how to interpret any experiences they may have whilst sitting. Each will need to keep a level head and not attach ideas to anything that might happen, until it is proven beyond reasonable doubt.

6. Circle leader

One among you may be chosen to be the leader of the circle. This person need not be a medium, although you may know of an established medium whom you can trust, who will be willing to act as a leader. The circle leader must be of sound mind: he or she will have a great influence on how the circle and sitters develop. For the sake of the group and the spirit, the leader must possess compassion, honesty of character, fairness and sensitivity to people. If possible, the circle leader should also possess a basic grounding in spiritual matters and development.

7. Harmony and trust

Most important of all is that the sitters get on well, trust one another, and encourage one another to grow in knowledge and understanding of the spirit.

8. Proceeding with development

In the beginning, sit once a week, for one hour only. Do not be tempted to sit for any longer, unless directed by the circle leader or by the spirit or unless all the sitters agree that a longer period would be useful.

You will need to learn how to be still, receptive and open. This is why meditation is of use to you. You will need to be non-judgemental during the period of sitting. Only when the circle has finished and closed in prayer will it be appropriate to analyse constructively what took place during the circle, how each sitter felt, what may or may not have occurred, etc. But even here you need to keep an open mind.

When you sit for development, your thoughts and prayers should surrender to the influence of the spirit world, so that the all-pervading power of the spirit may awaken and unfold within you.

In the initial stages you must develop silence, inwardly and outwardly, so that you learn how to relax the body and keep still, and breathe in a natural, relaxed manner without strain. You will then notice that as your body and breathing harmonise, your thoughts will start to slow down, your mind become calm and a feeling of peace pervade your being. This provides the spirit world with the right conditions to start the process of your development. At this stage you cannot do very much yourself, except to be open and receptive to all that may happen.

Dos and don'ts

1 Do take note of the feelings that occur, for example floating, facial or cobweb sensations, light bands around the head, bodily heaviness, changes in the rhythm of breathing, desire to stand, desire to speak, spinning sensations, seeing light, or the feeling of presences – the impression of a person, male or female, tall or short, strong or frail, etc. Be aware of anything that feels different from the normal. Let these feelings and sensations express themselves.

2 Do not interfere, but allow events to happen naturally. You do not know at this stage whether a sensation is due to a spirit personality, to the body relaxing, or to the effect of a change in your breathing pattern. Your aim is to see what is happening, so keep an open mind.

3 Do enjoy, in a relaxed way, all that happens to you, even if it is just a feeling of being relaxed in body and mind.

4 Do not be nervous about anything that happens. Nothing can or will harm you. Just continue to be calm, relaxed and at peace.

5 Do remember that the spirit are trying to make themselves known through your psychic senses. Realise that they have to work through our mind and consciousness so their task is difficult. Learn to be patient.

6 Do not be quick to judge any experience as being genuine or imaginary, or any appearance as being your guide or this or that spirit personality, until you are all sure, beyond reasonable doubt, that it is so. This point is of great importance as psychic and mediumistic sensitivity can make people very impressionable. Keep a level head at all times.

7 Do remember that you will go through some very peculiar experiences. The more familiar you become with them, the greater your understanding, responsiveness and sensitivity will be. You will also expand the range of your unfoldment.

The circle's motive

The best advice for anyone starting a circle is to have plenty of patience. Be prepared to sit and let the power of the spirit build. Do not try to force it. This is why it is important to choose your group of sitters carefully in order that there will be no friction, physically, mentally or spiritually. You must all have a common aim and interest.

A very important aspect of successful circle work is motive. Ask yourself what the motive is behind your desire to develop. It would not be advisable to sit if all you want to do is play about with psychic powers, as this is not enough for the spirit. Your motive must be about *selfless service*. If it is, you will find that you will develop greater qualities. The spirit seeks to help us rediscover our spiritual powers, which are and always have been inherent within us. But we need to be receptive and willing to develop ourselves for this to happen.

Go quietly about your work. Remember that your prevailing attitude of mind and approach will attract the corresponding influence around you and your circle so keep a check on your motives and your circle's motive for sitting.

Understand the importance of what you are undertaking. Mediumship is about many different things – not just phenomena. It is concerned with the soul's growth within the individual. It is about developing a deeper sense of responsibility to one's fellow human beings, and a greater commitment to truth and its dissemination. It is about understanding the spiritual laws that govern all aspects of life, and seeking, from within ourselves and from the spirit, the nature of these laws and how to implement them into our lives and work. If we really want to do something worthwhile, it must have a higher purpose. Remember that no time spent in searching for truth is ever wasted.

We see from this that our efforts will enable each of us to unfold a richer quality of life and living, physically and spiritually. We can then lead by example. Through that, the all-pervading power of God and spirit may touch and work through us in order to reach others.

*   *   *

A personal realisation

I am a perfect and receptive instrument for the spirit. I am guided by a Higher Power that expresses Itself in and through all that I do.

Mediumistic Powers

*I realise that all is part of the One, and that
the One is expressing Itself through all things.*

This chapter and the two that follow will deal with various classifications of mental mediumship. We hope they will give some understanding of the many facets of mental mediumship, which can be listed under nine headings:

(1) Clairvoyance
(2) Clairaudience
(3) Clairsentience
(4) Inspirational speaking
(5) Inspirational writing
(6) Inspirational drawing
(7) Automatic writing
(8) Automatic drawing
(9) Varying stages of trance

It should be noted that certain types of spiritual healing can come under the heading of mediumship as they can require someone to act as an intermediate or medium between the person seeking healing and the spirit world.

Subjective clairvoyance

Clairvoyance manifests itself and functions in two ways: subjectively and objectively. In subjective clairvoyance, the medium sees pictures that are impressed upon the mind. These pictures are recognised as thoughts conveyed by a person in the spirit world.

Spirit persons can project pictures not only of their features, build, manner of standing, etc., but also of objects relating to them from when they were living in the physical world. Many subjective clairvoyants liken this way of seeing to looking at a photograph in the mind. They may also subjectively see, and describe seeing, written words, such as names, places, etc. All this is perceived by the medium through the subjective consciousness. Yet our own minds and our ability to visualise play a role here in enabling the spirit world to impress us through the unconscious, so that images will impinge themselves upon the conscious mind. This will create a sense of seeing.

Objective clairvoyance

Objective clairvoyance is a form of mediumship through which a medium objectively sees spirit people, objects and other manifestations of a psychic nature by means of the psychic senses that function through the physical mechanism of vision. Without this, the objective states of clairvoyance would not be possible. But although there may be the *impression* of seeing a spirit person visibly with the physical eyes, this is not so, because a spirit entity is not a physical individual. We see spirit personalities with our psychic eyes.

Remember that the range and ability of both types of clairvoyance are governed by the rate of vibration in which they operate through us. Thus, one clairvoyant may see things that another does not because of the degree of difference in the necessary psychic power and its intensity.

Some objective clairvoyants also possess what is known as X-ray clairvoyance. This is the ability to see objects through intervening physical matter. Clairvoyants with this ability can view the inner parts of the human body, diagnose disease and see the actual processes of healing and decay.

Trance clairvoyance

Trance clairvoyance occurs when a spirit person assumes control of the medium's consciousness. At this point, the spirit in control becomes the actual clairvoyant transmitter. The spirit may use the medium's consciousness as the means to communicate information about themselves or other spirit personalities that are passing on information to them. They may give a philosophical talk. The question of whether the medium is an objective or subjective clairvoyant does not arise, as it is a discarnate spirit control, and not the medium, that has taken over the proceedings.

Telepathic and other types of clairvoyance

Telepathic clairvoyance also has a subjective and objective state and has to do with the clairvoyant seeing events happening to those still living.

There is also something termed 'travelling clairvoyance'. In this, the medium may be aware of being present at and seeing events that happened in the past, or events occurring in the present or future. This type of clairvoyance can also be perceived in a subjective or objective manner.

There is another type of clairvoyance that functions without the intervention of the spirit world. This is when information is perceived through the mind of the clairvoyant and through his or her own psychic perception, in either a subjective or objective manner.

Clairaudience

Clairaudience is the ability to hear spirit voices in either the subjective or objective states. Highly developed clairaudients will be able to identify voices as being male or female, young or old. They are able to describe them with all their inflections and accents. They can hear voices speaking in languages which are not their own and which they may be unfamiliar with, but they will be able to convey this information to the recipient. They often use phrases like 'They are telling me', or 'I hear them say', which indicates that they are hearing clairaudiently.

In the case of hearing objectively, the effects of the spirit voice may be so real as to make one believe that one is really hearing an audible physical voice. But this is not so, because it is not a physical voice. The physical ears do not actually hear them. As with objective clairvoyance, it works through the psychic senses, giving the *impression* of a physical voice, often described by the clairaudient as 'hearing in the head'.

One way to go about developing this faculty is to adopt an inner attitude of listening, and to remain expectant that one may hear something.

Clairsentience

This is the ability to sense and feel things about a spirit person. It functions on both the subjective and objective levels. We may describe impressions we receive through clairsentience as a feeling or sensing of a spirit person being of a certain height or build. We may sense and feel their character and personality. We may feel and sense what type of work they did, what part of the country they lived in, what colour their eyes and hair are, etc. This happens inwardly, as though we intuitively know these things about the person.

In this state the medium could have a feeling of becoming that person in an almost physical way, and exhibit the stance, mannerisms or other physical characteristics of the communicator. They might experience the sensation of loss of a limb, and even adopt the person's mental attributes and characteristics. As these occurrences function through the psychic senses, and act through the physical mechanism of sense and feeling, they represent a psychic, rather than spiritual, state of sensing and feeling.

*   *   *

A personal realisation

I am in tune with the spirit universe. I am in perfect harmony with all of God's creations. Divine intelligence runs through me, revitalising and awakening me to its dynamic presence.

Inspiration

*Free the spirit within me. Teach me how to know
and attain the way to unbounded and limitless potential.*

In mediumistic development, we often find a sense of being impelled, without reason, to speak or to act. External thoughts flow into our minds. These emanate from a source often beyond ourselves. But because thoughts and words are forms with which we are familiar, doubts may arise as to whether these are our own, or come from another source.

Do not forget that in all aspects of mediumistic development, the spirit have to use the equipment that we supply them with – they have to work with and through us.

In the initial stages of development, the spirit will have to break through our conscious and unconscious minds and learn how to influence the flow of thoughts entering into our conscious minds.

They may have no means of vocalising their thoughts. They have to use the mechanism of our minds in order to do so. Therefore, we need to adopt an open and trusting attitude towards the flow of thoughts that come into our consciousness, and over a period of time watch and observe, so that we will be able to see and give spirit time to make all the necessary adjustments they need to prove to us that inspiration is really coming from the spirit world.

Inspirational speaking

If at any time while sitting in a development circle you feel inspired to speak or stand up, do so. We suggest that you record everything that is said, so that over a period of time, you can look back and listen to or read what has been said and see if any changes have occurred in the manner of speech and the content and use of words.

However, we should remember that we are inspired not only by the spirit, but by what happens to us in our daily lives. Because we are spirit ourselves, inspiration can surface through our conscious mind. This too is a valid form of inspiration and plays as much of a part in our psychic development as spirit inspiration. Here again, the only way to develop this is to observe and look at every aspect of what happens. This can give insight into the many different levels that may inspire us, such as the spirit world, nature, music, art, literature, conversation, poetry, etc., and insight into how they affect our awareness of these levels.

Inspiration is a power that can stir the soul. Its value in development must never be underestimated. So follow through everything with an open and objective mind, and all should go well.

Inspirational writing

All that has been said about inspirational speaking applies to the impulse to write. Keep your mind open and do not allow yourself to prejudge what words may follow from others. Try to develop a broad, non-dogmatic attitude of mind.

Whatever information may come through, whether for yourself or another, look for evidence or proof of who is communicating. *Do not blindly accept any claim made.* If the information is philosophic, examine its content, and remember the role your own mind can play in this form of development.

Some people may unfold the skill to write poetry. Again you must examine the source from which it is coming: is it from you or from an individual spirit personality?

Inspirational drawing

Some may find themselves inspired to draw, even though they may lack artistic skills. Yet through spirit inspiration they may find that they are able to draw proficiently. At first the drawings may be crude in quality. But with patience and persistence they might develop into something exceptional, such as accurate renderings of faces of friends, relatives or helpers who have passed over to the spirit world. You need to look at the accuracy and the likeness of the drawing to the person depicted. Through this you will hopefully establish the reality of survival in the spirit world.

Some people develop the ability to draw the aura. They are often impressed or inspired to put certain colours on to paper. This may be for the purpose of analysing a person's character and potential, spiritually and physically. Again, records should be kept for its accuracy from the early stages to its more developed form.

With this type of development, and with all the above categories of inspiration, it is best to keep a level head and not make claims that it is coming from the spirit world or any particular personality until you have enough *evidence* that it really is.

Automatic writing

With the development of automatic writing, some may experience the sensation of minor electrical impulses going down their arm, and feel as though their hand no longer belongs to them. People developing this ability might ask for a pen to be placed in their hands as they feel that someone wishes to write through them.

If these feelings persist, allow them to continue and watch for any results. In the early stages, the writing is often just squiggles and swirls, almost childish in style. Those who wish to know more about this subject will find further information in *Spirit Teachings* by the Rev. William Stainton Moses, and in books by automatic writing medium Geraldine Cummins, which show some of the possibilities and types of material that can be produced through automatic writing.

When writing, the arm and hand may move automatically. But what actually causes this movement is by no means obvious or easy to explain.

Through a process of suggestion, we can remove control of our conscious minds and therefore allow a communicating spirit to take temporary hold through the mechanisms of our unconscious minds and brains, which controls the various nerves, movements and muscles of our bodies. It is through this that automatic writing is able to take place. It will, however, depend upon the degree to which we can control the influence of our conscious minds, which may in turn affect the message and its interpretation.

If our consciousness is not entirely removed, there will be a blending of our thoughts with those of the spirit. So here we must consider two factors: the mind of the spirit and the mind of the medium. A state of trance may be more desirable to eliminate the influence of the medium's conscious mind. Yet even in the different states of trance, the unconscious mind *will* and *can* affect the message and its interpretation to a greater or lesser degree. This is why it is important that we do not develop narrow or set ideas about mediumship and its development, as our minds and the range of our thoughts are potentially so vast.

Thoughts may come from the unconscious. This brings a third factor into consideration: unconscious control. We therefore suggest that as this aspect of mediumship develops, the medium is blindfolded or asked to sit in a darkened room to proceed with the writing. Afterwards, any material produced should be removed so that the medium does not see it, and the content and style of writing examined. This will help towards excluding any unconscious reproduction of work.

One should proceed with this form of test until the medium and the sitters are satisfied that it is discarnate information, and is both reliable and consistent. Other tests in lighted conditions can then be introduced.

The medium and the sitters must always question what level the information is coming from. In all aspects of mediumship, we need satisfactory evidence that it emanates from a source beyond ourselves. This is why it is important to proceed slowly. We should not be in a hurry to do things for which we may not be ready.

*   *   *

A personal realisation

I am open to receive and be impressed by the creative mind of the Spirit.

Trance

Make me one with Your eternal goodness.
Help me to serve with an open mind
and a compassionate heart.

There are numerous degrees of trance, ranging from a state of feeling inspired by a discarnate spirit personality to deep unconsciousness. The latter brings about a temporary suspension of ordinary consciousness to external surroundings. In this state, the medium takes on and displays the character, personality and mannerisms of the controlling spirit. This occurs through the mind only – the spirit does not inhabit the body. It is through the mind that the spirit controls the mechanisms of the body: heartbeat, breathing, speech, etc. In this state, the spirit can even walk the medium about in a normal manner, with the eyes shut or blindfolded. This demonstrates that a discarnate spirit does not need to use the medium's physical sense of sight to move around.

The effect of trance on a medium

The conscious and unconscious minds will register thoughts from a controlling spirit. This may subsequently influence the conscious thought process of a medium in his or her normal life, spiritual life, and attitude towards development.

Trance can be used as a means by which the spirit can influence and unfold within the medium the ability to become a finer instrument for the dissemination of spiritual truths. But we must not think that this form of spirit education is the ultimate aim of our spiritual growth.

Trance in its finest form can help us to enhance our finer qualities as well as refine the more negative aspects of our natures, but only if we are prepared to work on ourselves and discover how we can best develop our spiritual natures and be open to creative influences.

Trance, as in all forms of mediumship, is about co-operation. All forms of mediumship, particularly trance, should heighten *every* level of a medium's perception, not just the psychic and mediumistic. If mediums allow trance to affect them in this way, the influence of a controlling spirit will filter into their unconscious and affect their conscious minds. This will then heighten and expand their normal conscious states of perception.

Stages of trance

All spirit influence is actually a form of trance. All mediums, whether demonstrating normal clairvoyant, clairaudient or clairsentient mediumship, or speaking inspirationally, are in a state of entrancement. Even though the mediums remain aware of all that is happening, a certain part of their minds will be controlled and influenced by a spirit personality in order to express information.

In the early stages of development we may feel sensations such as heaviness, cobweb-type feelings, tight bands across the head and body, tingling sensations on the head and face and numerous other parts of the body, which *may* or *may not* indicate spirit activity and influence.

Types of entrancement

There are varying light, overshadowing states of trance where the medium experiences the desire to speak, but feels that the words are coming from an outside source. What should be looked for in this type of mediumship is the quality of information and how it is expressed, i.e. whether or not there is a continuity of expression that would indicate the spirit's presence, such as philosophy which displays a high degree of knowledge, or concrete information which can be verified as unknown to the medium.

In the deeper states of overshadowing, mediums experience less control and selectivity of the information given through them. Though they may be aware of what is being said, they find that they are not able to control the information. They hear themself speak, but are unable to perceive what they are actually saying. This might indicate the possibility of a deeper state yet to be developed.

In this section we have mentioned only a few of the actual stages of trance, the degrees of which may vary from one person to another.

Development of trance

Because we know so little about the human mind and its spiritual counterpart, it is difficult to be precise about how each potential trance medium should proceed with his or her development. This is where idealism, trust and spiritual aspiration will play their part. We must never forget that although the same Power operates through us all, the actual result of that Power has to manifest through our individuality and all aspects of our character, personality and mind.

The development of trance requires patience and the ability to be still, bodily and mentally, so that we may enter into a state of silence, through which we withdraw our conscious mind from all outer activity to an inner state of consciousness. This should be accompanied by a responsiveness to all that may happen during the time we sit. We must open ourselves to respond to whatever spirit influences register upon our consciousness.

This state of withdrawal will quicken our psychic and spiritual senses, and allow these senses to ebb and flow in such a way that helps our minds to become aware of, and responsive to, the spirit's presence and influence. Through this the possibility for entrancement will intensify.

Because there are many factors that will determine the rate of trance development, it is not possible to give any definite time in which this aspect of mediumship can be developed. One's objective must be to meet the spirit halfway and enter into reciprocal and conscious co-operation with them.

Circle sitters

We now come to the role that circle sitters play in the development of trance mediumship. Regularity and punctuality are essential. All sitters are required first of all to be level-headed and not inclined to jump to conclusions. They must be able to distinguish fact from fantasy, and be willing to devote their time and power to the development of a potential trance medium. The sitters should not try to accomplish this by means of force, but by patience and accepting that the spirit may use whatever power they need to quicken the development of the medium in the direction that they wish his or her development to go.

The sitters may observe certain changes occurring to the medium which could indicate the development of entrancement. The medium may jerk or experience vibratory, trembling sensations, and report temporary loss of physical sensations. The medium might afterwards describe pricking sensations, like mild electric shocks, or a feeling of wanting to stand and speak. Everything that happens should be accepted calmly and rationally, with no time limit, presupposition or restriction placed upon what is happening or when it will be developed. At all times the medium should be encouraged to carry on working until the stage comes when the spirit proves itself. When it does, the spirit may be asked for further direction and guidance for the circle.

With the unfoldment of trance, and with all psychic and mediumistic abilities, perseverance is essential. In the initial stages, there is often very little to show for the efforts put in by the individuals of the circle. Nonetheless, dedication and perseverance will eventually bring rewards.

Remember that this is an experiment by you and the spirit world, and that both sides of life are endeavouring to co-operate. Therefore, we must not be discouraged by what could appear to be failure or by any long periods of inactivity as we may never know what our efforts might have achieved and what changes brought about. Instead, we must persevere and approach circle work as an act of dedication and selfless service to humanity and to the spirit.

Do not let disturbing or discordant thoughts or disappointments affect the finer vibrations of the spirit. Mediums are sensitive: these can have an adverse effect upon their sensitivity and progress. It is for this reason that harmony of thought and attitude in all aspects of development should be aimed for. Without it, successful development cannot be accomplished.

Trance in mental mediumship

In mental mediumship, trance may be used by the spirit control to address us upon matters of spiritual philosophy and teachings. These can be of a general nature for a public meeting, or of a more specific nature for an individual or group. It might be used in the private sitting, enabling the spirit control to pass on messages of more depth than may normally occur in other states of mediumship. Departed relatives belonging to a sitter may entrance a medium and give evidence of survival.

Trance can be used in mental mediumship for the public demonstration of trance speaking and trance clairvoyance. In general, trance in mental mediumship is confined to the small group, circle, or private sitting. It is better for mediums to be guided by spirit friends in the use of this aspect of mediumship, as they will know more about the development of this type of mediumship and how best to use it.

Trance in physical mediumship

Trance in physical mediumship is used to enable the spirit world to work with energies necessary for the production of physical phenomena, such as direct voice, materialisation and apports. Yet we know little of what these energies are and what is entailed in their production. At times these energies may be visible, as in ectoplasm or small pin-pricks of light. They may also be experienced by the sitters in the form of a sudden change in the atmosphere or temperature of the room.

After being entranced, the medium may experience sensations of discomfort in the region of the solar plexus or in the throat, or notice a general feeling of debility because the medium's life force has been used during this state. The sitters too may note physical pullings or possible gurgling sounds from these areas. These occur because spirit personalities are extracting the energies that they need to carry out their work and to entrance the medium. Similar sensations may also be experienced in the development of trance in mental mediumship.

Energies used in this type of mediumship are a combination of those from the medium and the sitters. These are blended with energies from the spirit world and used to produce, vibrate and affect the atmosphere of our world. Through this, spirit personalities can build ectoplasmic structures and produce physical phenomena. However, the trance state is not always necessary for the production of such phenomena.

Spiritual perspective of trance

We have already said that trance, if rightly developed, can enhance and stimulate all the powers that we possess, both naturally and spiritually.

What we must realise is that the message of the spirit is about universal service. Therefore, we must hope to develop from these trance states a more universal and open outlook.

Mediums should allow the inspiring influences of the spirit to encourage them to transform any negatives within their character, such as jealousy, envy, suspicion, destructive criticism of self and others, and nurture more positive qualities which will help them face and overcome their negatives and free themselves from the power of their expression.

Try at all times to encourage a more expansive state of aspiration by means of prayer, quiet contemplation and meditation. Mediums must endeavour to practise these, as they will enhance further development. At no time should the mediums feel that they stand apart from the normal activity of daily life, but should try to incorporate their experiences into everyday living.

Mediums ought to endeavour to unfold and develop a closer union with God, nature and humankind. They should encourage within themselves a deeper creativity and appreciation of art, beauty, love and wisdom, as this will cultivate the mediums' minds and characters, which is what self-effort and self-development are about. This can only widen and deepen the influence of mediumistic potential and hopefully attract spirit helpers of wider knowledge. This will bring the mediums under the spirit's sphere of influence, resulting in a greater effect upon their mind, character, personality and spiritual growth. This in turn may prove the means by which the mediums become a greater influence for all that is good and true, and an example by which humankind may be led to understand its true nature and potential.

*   *   *

A personal realisation

My life is the limitless life of the Spirit.
My mind is full of harmonious peace.
My heart is filled with loving kindness.
My life is perfect and complete.

Physical Mediumship

Transform my consciousness so I may know of
no limitations and may awaken to greater things.

This area of mediumistic development deals with how the spirit world can use psychic energy and bring about materialisations of spirit personalities, dematerialise physical objects and rematerialise them again, or recreate the audible voice of a spirit through the use of a seance trumpet which amplifies the sound.

Through this type of mediumship the spirit world can build masks from ectoplasm for transfiguration, and, by using psychic energy, move and levitate physical objects as well as the human body. They can create odours and perfumes seemingly out of nothing and cause raps to be heard. They are able to bring about changes in a room's temperature and create visible lights and luminosity.

For those interested in knowing more about this type of mediumship, Leslie Flint's *Voices in the Dark*, and a recently republished book on materialisation by Harry Boddington, are recommended. Both cover the phenomena of materialisation and direct voice.

How to sit

For many years people sitting for the development of physical phenomena have sat in the dark. There is no reason why you should not do this and for any phenomena that occur to be genuine. But if you are going to invite strangers into your circle to witness phenomena that are developing, it is more advisable to sit under a good red light and thus disperse any doubts people may have about their validity.

In some circles there is a small table in the centre, and a cabinet, curtained off in the corner of the room, in which the medium may sit. However you decide to sit – whether seating someone in the cabinet, or sitting with hands on the table to develop table-tilting phenomenon – you must at all times look to the spirit for guidance on how to proceed with the development of the circle, through whatever means they may wish to communicate with you.

Sitting for the potential physical medium

If someone is already showing obvious signs of physical mediumship, the lead may be taken from this: sit for that person to see what may develop from it. When it is not known whether anyone has such potential, it is best to sit in a normal manner, with the intention that the spirit world will guide and eventually direct you all to sit for one particular person.

The reason you will be asked to sit for that one person is that all the energies – psychic, physical and mental – from you and the medium may be utilised for the development of physical mediumship. The spirit world will use these energies to experiment with the sensitivity of the medium and with the physical effects that may potentially occur.

Progress in the circle

In the early days the proceedings may be erratic, irregular and rather clumsy. This is why patience and an open mind on the part of all are essential. The sitters as well as the developing medium may have unusual experiences. It will take time for all – including the spirit world – to adjust to these changes. But whatever occurs, let it happen.

As development proceeds, the phenomena may take on varying forms (as mentioned in the beginning of this chapter). But we should always be looking to the spirit for reasons why the phenomena occur, and what value they have. The ultimate aim in this form of development is to prove survival after death, and that there are powers both within and beyond us that can control physical activity.

During development, various trance states may intervene. This will introduce the circle and the medium to those in the invisible world that will work with them. You may eventually come to know the various roles that they will play in the different phenomena that unfold. Once the spirit have established their presence, they will be able to instruct the circle how best to proceed at different stages of development.

Be open to the spirit's directions. If you feel that its instructions are sensible and practical, then follow them and see if it helps the medium and the circle to move forward in any way. Hopefully, events will go according to plan and the circle make noticeable progress. But if little appears to happen, go back to the spirit and seek an explanation. Do not just accept anything that is given to you as fact. Question everything that happens or is said – this is the safest procedure.

All those who develop these abilities will react to and develop them in individual ways because of their own psychic nature and the spirit influences that work through them. There are no hard and fast ways of developing these powers. All members of the group should proceed with care and caution, and not allow any public demonstration of these abilities until all reasonable doubt about the circle's and medium's development, and any phenomena produced, has been removed.

We should not forget that because we are spirit ourselves, objects can be moved, and all manner of physical phenomena occur through the use of mind-power, without the intervention of the spirit world. Parapsychologists and psychical researchers have noted that in certain altered states of consciousness, ectoplasmic substances can manifest themselves. Build-ups may occur without any form. But they have noticed that there is no evidence of a distinctly separate influence or mind during these occurrences.

We have to realise that in all forms of mediumistic development, the mediums are in a highly suggestible state, and that if we suggest things to them, they may well take them on board unconsciously. This is why it is important never to form or force opinions, but only to give a very broad outline and watch without any preconceived ideas. We can only prove beyond reasonable doubt, but prove we must, that these phenomena are influenced by a mind that is discarnate and separate from ours.

*   *   *

A personal realisation

I commit my life to the One Perfect Power that creates all.

Healing

Teach me how I may best serve You
and leave behind all thoughts of separation.

The purpose of this chapter is not to condone or condemn any particular form of healing, but to encourage the reader to be open to its infinite possibilities.

There are many forms of healing. Techniques include spirit healing, positive thought, prayer, absent healing and so on. Most methods appear to have their successes as well as failures. No one really knows why this happens. Some say it is to do with the patient's receptiveness to healing energies. An important factor is that the patient must *want* to get better. The effectiveness of healing may equally lie with the healer: with one's ability to be an instrument for healing and allowing a Greater Power to work properly and freely through one.

We should avoid laying the blame of non-healing at the door of the patient. The truth is that much of life is still a mystery. Just as we know that healing can relieve or cure, we also appreciate that there are times when it does not. Healing in many cases is about acceptance of things as they are, and making peace with ourselves and those around us, especially when it is nearing our time to leave this earthly existence.

Self-healing and the transpersonal element

Techniques of self-healing are also varied. Many people are turning to affirmative thought, hatha yoga and visualisation and meditation techniques. All can be valuable in the process of returning individuals to wholeness and health, or helping them accept an illness with a positive attitude.

It is quite common for people to experience an instantaneous healing without the aid of a healer or any self-healing techniques. This often appears to happen in a person's darkest hour. Such people, suffering from deep depression, perhaps near-suicidal feelings, may come to a point where they let go of all negative conditions, surrender, and allow room for *something else* to take over.

Such individuals usually experience a force outside themselves intervening and lifting their consciousness. They often feel united with an all-pervading Reality, which goes beyond the duality of appearances. A sense of timelessness is often experienced, and all problems seem to melt into insignificance. They may suddenly see the world as if for the first time, and view all as being part of One Complete Whole. They often feel and know that they, too, are part of all life. Some report seeing lights or spirit people, hearing voices, or having out-of-body experiences.

An all-embracing feeling of unconditional love usually accompanies these experiences, which seem to touch the very centre of one's being. Yet it is the change that occurs within the individual which is significant. A transformation often happens alongside the experience. The person's character and outlook upon life usually change for the better.

As some illnesses, both mental and physical, can be outward manifestations of inward trauma, such as stress, fear, worry, guilt, anxiety, etc., we can clearly see why this change in consciousness is important in healing. Life may not necessarily become any easier for individuals, but they may find the courage and conviction to face life with more understanding and acceptance.

Many of the experiences described above are consciously unsought and come when least expected. But there are cases where people have deliberately visited a particular site to seek a cure, and found it. Some have suddenly been restored to good health amidst the countryside or a natural scene of beauty. Animals also seem to have a healing effect on certain people. It is easy to understand why, as they can put us back in touch with our true senses and remind us that we are all interconnected with nature and the vastness of life around us.

Some have even prayed to images of holy men or women, and been healed. Yet none of these occurrences should be classed as unique to any single belief, as they all work through the use of the same universal law. It is only we who interpret that law differently and colour it with our own individual ideas and beliefs.

The Power that works through all

Various beliefs and theories have built up around the practice of healing. One would think that healing would unite everyone in the common cause for good. Yet some practitioners claim the results of their work to be proof that only their way is right, and condemn others because their beliefs, methods or views are different. Some maintain that others are working with the wrong energies. This is not true, as the same power operates through all. We may, however, have distorted the use of that power by imposing restrictions on how it operates.

Whether we call this power, 'spirit-energy', 'the vital force', or 'cosmic intelligence', it emanates from the same source. It is the very essence of life itself, permeating everything in the universe. It is the substance, continuity, activity and reality of all creation.

Confusion often arises in understanding this power when people expect it to work solely for those who view it as an expression or sign of their own beliefs. But this is not the way it operates, for it is indiscriminate, available for all. Some may try to place labels on it, but it will not make its use exclusive to anyone.

Whatever method of healing you use, let it be the means by which you discover this truth for yourself. Although healing is not accomplished by simply acquiring knowledge of the truth, it nonetheless helps us reach that goal, and leads us to conscious union with that Power that is God.

As you turn within and relax in the realisation of your oneness with God, with spirit, and with God as your individualised being and identity, it will manifest itself outwardly as a demonstration of that unity. When you start to understand the many ways in which spirit-energy functions, you will begin to shed old beliefs that have kept you from recognising this Power, for it is both a learning and unlearning process which brings you closer to truth.

In touch with the perfect Self

The purpose of healing is to restore health, balance and harmony to those who are in need. Though the ways in which this can be brought about are many, the underlying principle is the same.

Acknowledge that you are a perfect expression of the One Reality

(God). It seeks expression in you, as you, and works through you at your current level of understanding. As a deeper understanding of this Reality is reached, it will manifest itself more fully within you. It will then work in and through you to a greater, less limited degree.

Your receptiveness to this power is your responsibility. If you keep yourself open to its influence, you will become a greater instrument for its demonstration. But be aware that it is not through personal will-power that healing is brought about, but by the interaction of God and spirit restoring any imbalance.

Because God's and the spirit's power has to function through our mind and consciousness, the more open-minded we are, the more free-flowing it will be. Let us not place any finite appearance at the door of the Infinite, because if we judge by appearances, we will become bound by them.

Leave behind all beliefs which may limit this power and have trust in it. Just as when switching on a light you know it will release enough electricity to light up a room, so, too, trust and know that the universal power of God and spirit will do the work. Even leave all thoughts and ideas of healing aside, and quietly be aware of that power. This is what healers mean when they talk of 'getting themselves out of the way'. So do not concern yourself with appearances. Consider the fact that many people may go to a healer with the same particular complaint, yet the causes might be totally different.

If you are giving healing to someone for a specific problem, the last thing on your mind should be any thought that reinforces the appearance of separation from God and spirit. Be free from beliefs that tie you to person, place or thing.

A healer once told us that he was short of time when giving healing to a group of people, and forgot to ask one woman what her problem was. The next day she told him that a condition no doctor had been able to cure had completely gone. We see from this that although healers may have the desire to see a person well, they need not concern themselves with the illness, but instead remain 'nonattached' to any outward appearance.

One healer, who achieves remarkable results through her healing work, always works with the power of love and never with any thought of illness or disharmony.

Working with the Power

Healers may be aware of energies working through them. Energy may be experienced leaving the solar plexus, or there may be feelings of something touching the crown of the head, of cold or heat emanating from the hands, or of uplifting thoughts. Some healers are said to have produced oil with a scented fragrance on their hands.

People being healed may also experience similar sensations of hot and cold, a change in the body's energies, or feel vibrations, movements or breezes around the body. They may start to feel very relaxed and drift off into a sleep-like state through which healing energies might have a greater effect. This may happen because they have let go of any worries or beliefs connected with any imbalance in the body and are allowing life-restoring healing energies to function more freely. In some cases, the healer and patient may experience nothing at all. But this does not mean that healing has not taken place.

Healers may develop other gifts that can be used alongside healing, such as clairvoyance or clairsentience, and use them for diagnosis, or even work in a light or deep trance state. They may be able to see or feel the aura, and see or feel where there is a blockage of the patient's life force, as it is through the aura that healing energies are said to work. But more important than the methods in which healers work is the result.

Attunement with the Universal Life Force

We should not take credit for any demonstration of healing. We do not use the Power, but merely let it work through us. Even to call ourselves healers is misleading as we are not the repairers of damage or restorers of harmony: that is the function of God and spirit.

Let us view healing as a means of dedication and service and go about our work quietly, unselfishly and 'nonattached', knowing that it is the Power that is God and spirit, recognised and realised, which does the work. Let us also realise that this Power functions through all and is Perfect. It is the maintaining Force in all life, and seeks to express Itself through our own being. This does not mean that we suppress or deny our problems. It is simply a matter of letting go and allowing God to take over.

We can attune ourselves to be more open to this influence by means of prayer, affirmation and meditation, and surrendering to a state of silent receptivity where we give ourselves over to that Power so that it may work freely within us and through us.

A balanced outlook on life is essential as well as devotion to high ideals, for these will refine and enhance our spiritual awareness. Those of compassionate, caring and unselfish natures will obviously be more attuned to healing work.

Remember that you are not just a centre of consciousness *in*, but are an individualised expression *of*, the One Power. Do not place any preconceived ideas upon what that Power can or cannot do. Just let It be and let go of any idea or concept that may create the appearance of separation from It.

*　　*　　*

Opening to the Universal Power

The following is a list of negatives and positives which create either the appearance of separation from the universal Power that is God and spirit, or awaken you to knowing your true relationship with It, so hindering or helping you in recognising It in all things and all people – including yourself.

Negatives which create the appearance of separation from God and spirit	*Positives which help us become more aware and reflect our true relationship with God and spirit*
Anger and hatred	*Love and compassion*
Living other people's lives	*Living our own lives the best we can*
Prejudice and judging those who are different from us	*Unity and acceptance of the lives of others*
Selfishness and separation from others	*Selflessness and connecting with all life*
Superiority and indifference	*Giving oneself and being there for others*
Arrogant, irrational and uncontrolled behaviour	*Composure, balance and self-mastery*
Rigid and narrow views	*Openness of mind and thought*
Inflexibility and stagnation	*Flexibility and growth*

Spiritual pride and self-importance	Self-awareness and humility
Self-criticism	Self-acceptance
Inferiority	Realising our potential
Delusion	Seeing things as they are
Ingratitude and receiving without thanks	Thankfulness and awakening to the good we have
Ill-will, greed and deviousness	Goodwill, kindness and good intentions
Injustice and deception	Fairness and truthfulness
Confusion and doubt	Clear and intuitive thinking
Uncaring and mindless conduct	Caring and mindful actions
Disrespect	Positive regard for all
Impatience and hostility	Tolerance and patience
Agitation and conflict	Peacefulness and contentment
Thoughtlessness and vindictiveness	Awareness and forgiveness
Fear and anxiety	Faith and trust
Beliefs grounded in superstition and ignorance	Beliefs grounded in truth and wisdom
Depression and worry	Wholeness and healing
Suppressed and blocked emotions	Open to life, joy and happiness
Denying our feelings	Letting in and accepting
Holding on to negative appearances	Letting go and letting God

Exercises

I am one with all the Creative Power in the universe.

These visualisation techniques will aid you in developing deeper concentration, and psychic and mediumistic powers. They can be safely practised alone or in a development group. These exercises will help develop awareness and sensitivity:

1   Either lie on the floor on your back, or sit keeping the spine erect. Become aware of each part of your body in turn: the palms of your hands, backs of your hands, your fingers, feet, toes, ankles, calf muscles, knees, thighs, hamstrings, buttocks, back, shoulders, chest, arms, elbows, neck and head. Be aware of any tension. Wherever you find tension, let go of it as you exhale. Surrender it with your out-breath.

2   Turn your attention to your breathing. Find your normal rhythm of breathing, then visualise your whole body lying down or sitting (whatever position you are in) in the room as you are. See it completely relaxed and tranquil. As you are visualising this, become aware of feeling warm. Then imagine yourself becoming hot. Try to create this sensation and feel it as you would on a summer's day.

3   Now reverse the feeling. Try to feel cold, shivering cold, as you would on an icy day, in a bitter wind. Try to feel how chilled you would be. Feel this cold with conscious effort.

4   Next create the feeling of heaviness in your physical body. Imagine your body becoming heavier and heavier. Feel that you are unable to move any part of your body, even your eyelids. You are not even able to wiggle your toes or fingers because your body has become so heavy.

5   Reverse the feeling and experience the body becoming light. Feel the body becoming lighter and lighter until it is completely weightless. Imagine your body being so light that it is like a piece of cotton.

Do all this quite quickly with your thought. Do not take too long in trying, but just let the experience happen. Work on this practice until you can do it with concentration and intensity as this will help you to be more sensitively aware of different feelings.

After you become proficient in this, you can visualise yourself holding different objects. For instance, see yourself (in your mind's eye) holding a piece of wood or cloth. Feel the texture of it within your hands, the length, the roughness or smoothness, the colour and so on. Imagine and feel the sensation of the chosen object. See yourself holding it. But use only your imagination and not the physical object. You can also use colour or combinations of colour. Ask yourself how you feel about a certain colour and try to analyse your feelings.

You can even visualise yourself talking to someone you know. See yourself chatting and then see them talking to you. As the conversation develops in your mind, analyse the sensations you are experiencing. Try to feel what mood the conversation is in. If you are laughing, try to feel this laughter within yourself. See yourself talking to someone you have met for the first time. Try to feel the mood of the conversation. Then visualise someone you do not like and note your reactions.

Another exercise of this type is to visualise someone you have known who has passed on to the spirit world. But in this instance, try to let your mind be open to what may come from them. As the experience occurs, listen and see the person. In listening, capture and feel into what they are saying. As you look at them, ask yourself questions about them: are they as you remember? Are they younger or older? Does there appear to be anything different about them? Try to use your psychic and mediumistic abilities to become more aware of these impressions. Notice whether it is a genuine experience or just an impression conjured up by your imagination. See if you can distinguish a difference.

In practising these various techniques, you will be training your mind and finer senses to become more responsive. You will be teaching your sensitivity to react to non-physical things in a much more positive way so that when you seek communication of the spirit, you will be able to respond more strongly to its influence.

Practise each exercise stage-by-stage, but do not rush. Realise that it is you who is visualising. Do not accept any experience you have during these exercises as being of a genuine psychic or mediumistic nature until you are absolutely sure and have evidence that it is so.

The purpose of visualisation exercises

Visualisation techniques are important as they can widen our creative consciousness. They also provide the spirit world with more means through which they can work, as it is via the mind that they communicate. This is why artists can often make natural subjective clairvoyants because of their ability to visualise internally.

It is important to note that in conveying messages to and through us, the spirit can – and often will – use images that are strongly associated with things within our life and memory. For instance, you may regularly be given the impression of your mother or father as a symbol with which you can identify. It does not mean that the spirit world are necessarily saying that it is *your* mother or father communicating, but is a way of telling you that it is the parent of a person to whom you might be conveying information.

Visualisation exercise in attunement

An important stage in development is the link that we have with our spirit guides and helpers. The technique of visualisation we are going to describe is a means by which we can open our consciousness, so that contact and communication with these spirit beings may be possible. It should be practised with a totally open mind, with no preconceptions as to what may or may not come. Therefore it must be treated only as an experiment.

This exercise is a creative visualisation in attunement. Even if you do not experience anything, it will help you to build up your powers of attunement with the spirit:

1   Sit in a chair in an upright position (or in your preferred meditation position) and find your natural rhythm of breathing.

2 Consciously relax your body, then say a quiet prayer, seeking the aid of the Great Power and the spirit to help you in this endeavour.

3 In your mind's eye, visualise yourself going to a location of your own choice, perhaps a favourite place that you know, a garden or somewhere that you can easily visualise.

4 As you enter this place, find a seat to sit on. Feel relaxed, calm and happy about the possibility of meeting those in the spirit world who work with you. Be aware that you are going to meet someone or some people from the spirit world.

5 Keep relaxed and wait for the event to unfold. If it does not, do not worry as you can try again another time. But it is important at this point to keep the mind open and not conjure up images, hopes or aspirations in your own mind.

6 While sitting in this place, ask yourself what feelings you have. If someone appears to you, question what is happening, for example is the person talking to you, or are you talking to them? Is the dialogue mind-to-mind or verbal? Check every detail in your mind as well as the reality of the experience and the impact it has upon you. Are you receiving any instructions or guidance? Try to take note of every detail concerning this experience.

7 As you approach the end of the exercise, ask whether this is a genuine experience or not. If you feel that it is, ask the person to prove to you that they are really there.

8 As the visualisation comes to an end, return with a feeling of joy, peace and serenity – really feel these emotions. Come back to yourself and sit quietly for a few moments so that the experience becomes grounded in your being. Acknowledge that you have taken a step in building your link with the spirit. Try each day to keep the feeling alive within you. Keep yourself open and receptive to unfoldment.

As you develop your contact and communication with the spirit world, you can develop visual mind journeys. For example, when communicators come to you, ask them where they lived and to take you there. Be aware of the locations and their homes. Let them show you the outside and the inside. Look for information that could be confirmed, like nameplates or numbers on the doors, or the names of streets. Learn to ask the spirits questions appertaining to their lives and their passing from this earth. Seek their names and surnames, and ask about them and others whom they have since met in the spirit world.

You must learn how to probe with your mind so that you build between yourself and the spirit a dialogue of thought, vision, sound, feeling and sensing. Do not limit the capability of receiving information by having any preconceived notions or set views about what might happen. Have confidence in yourself, but keep checking to see if the information is correct. But do not force anything. Just be open, receptive and aware.

Description exercises

In the demonstration of clairvoyance, clairaudience and clairsentience, the clarity of description plays an integral part. It is therefore important to develop the ability to interpret clearly and describe accurately what one sees, hears or feels, as this will help develop the quality of one's mediumship.

Although the following mental exercises have nothing to do with psychic or mediumistic activity, they will help you develop the ability to describe certain things more accurately. The exercises are designed to help you to use natural means of description to convey specific information. You will find that this will be of great value when it comes to conveying any mediumistic information:

Description exercise 1

1 Ask a friend to sit with you and describe someone who is known to you both, but without saying their name. Try to describe this person's character, personality, sex, age, height, hair, build, manner, dress, distinguishing features, etc. See if your friend can recognise the person you are describing.

2 Detail, without naming, an area of a town or place known to you and your friend. Outline its main features, for example whether it is an area of a city or countryside. Describe any buildings, road layout, etc., and see if your friend can recognise the place.

109

3 Describe to your friend, without naming them, various types of objects in common everyday use, especially ones known to you both, which may be associated with people you know. Do not name the objects and see if your friend can identify them from your descriptions.

Description exercise 2

Listen to music of various types, or read poetry, descriptive novels or non-fiction, such as books on nature, art or history. Notice how you feel as you read or listen, and write down your feelings so that you remember them. This will help you to describe things that are more abstract, which can often come into spirit communication.

Description exercise 3

Describe to a friend various emotions and feelings without saying what they are. Afterwards ask your friend to tell you what they thought you were describing, and to point out where they feel you may have been unclear in your description.

Psychic and mediumistic experiments

In each of the following three experiments, start by placing yourself in a calm and relaxed frame of mind. Try to be as descriptive as possible. Afterwards analyse all the information that comes to you, and determine how subjective or objective the information was.

Bear in mind that impressions or images of a symbolic nature may come, which you will have to probe in order to discover their true meaning. At first it may not be obvious that the impression or image is symbolic. The following observation by Santoshan illustrates this:

> I once subjectively saw a monk, which at first seemed to represent a spirit communicator or guide. It was only after analysing this image and seeing how it looked more like a caricature than a real person that I realised it was a way of telling me that someone was connected with the surname of Monk. On the same occasion I was shown lipstick being applied. This was a way of conveying the surname of Yardley.

We see from these examples that it is necessary to probe any impressions or images and work with them, as one's first and more obvious interpretations can sometimes be wrong. This is why it is important to ask questions like, 'Why am I being shown this?' and 'What does it mean?'. If you fail to do this, you may miss some important evidential information, and what you give as evidence could be incorrect. There may be times when what you perceive appears to be wrong, but what is really incorrect is your interpretation.

Experiment 1

1   Ask a friend to sit in a chair opposite you.

2   Put aside all that you know about this friend. Try to sense that friend physically. Find out information about his or her physical life without asking any questions. This could be related to your friend's character or work, or to the people with whom he or she works. Find out any information that could be used to prove that you are obtaining these details through your psychic senses.

Experiment 2

This is a basic exercise in which persistence will prove beneficial. Remember that mistakes are as helpful as accuracy.

1   In this experiment, try to gain some information from the spirit world that links with your friend which proves survival after death. When seeking this communication, try to be aware if you are seeing. If so, describe whether you are seeing subjectively or objectively.

2   Try to be aware of the communicator speaking to you. Notice how you are sensing. If you receive any information pass it on to your friend. By doing this, you are bringing your friend into contact with all that is happening to you, and encouraging him or her to be an active participant.

Note: As we have asked you to choose friends in this experiment, it will be helpful to place all opinion and knowledge of them aside. You will find that doing this will help you to depend more on your psychic senses and on the spirit world's influence.

Experiment 3

1   Ask a friend to bring some objects belonging to someone they know, without telling you to whom they belong. Take one of them and try to sense and feel to whom it belongs. Ask yourself whether the person is a man or woman. Attempt to find out about the character of the person.

2   Now seek to find out if the person is still living or not. If they are in the spirit world, try to gain some evidence that will prove they are actually communicating with you. If they are still living, see if you can discover something that can be checked.

Note: Once you start to reach for some form of communication, we advise you to put the object down.

PART THREE

Synthesis

Cultivate awareness, acceptance and letting go.

Self-awareness

Divine Spirit of infinite wisdom,
help me to find You in the depths of my soul.
Show me how I may awaken to Your omnipresent love.

Many psychologists believe that the West is in spiritual crisis, that automation and rationalism have alienated many people from themselves, others and the natural world. Too much emphasis has been placed on external values instead of awakening to the unity we share with all life, finding inner peace, coming to terms with who and what we are, and cultivating a proper balance between body, mind, emotions, spirit and nature.

It is for this reason that the development and the harmonising of inner and outer awareness are important, as spiritual development entails cultivating inner awareness and bringing our emotions, thoughts and perceptions into harmony with all aspects of our outer lives.

Through inner awareness we can awaken to qualities of the true Self, bring down any barriers that we have created around our hearts and be more in tune with life around us. We can become more aware of our needs, our nature, and how life has moulded our current personalities and beliefs. With this comes the possibility of change and of unfolding various potentials. We can each transform our overall nature and the direction of our life, but only if we are willing to make the effort.

Creative choice and growth

We learn about life from the moment we are born. Each of us sees life from our individual standpoint. What we have so far experienced, learned, felt, thought and achieved has made us into what we are. Through trials and troubles we may have become more worldly individuals. But worldliness may not lead us to discover the truth about our own being. Indeed, it can lead us away from spiritual growth.

You may have observed that the effect of any unpleasant life experiences will not always help us deal appropriately with new ones, as we often let the outcome of such episodes influence us in a negative way. This can affect our judgement and cause us to react instead of being open and receptive to life. If we examine our perceptions and judgements we will find that some of them are the product of habit led by ingrained views and emotions.

We must endeavour to break free from anything that restricts us, and seek to understand life from a wider perspective. If we cultivate acceptance, an open heart and more positive qualities within us so that they interact with our emotions, thoughts and actions, we will be able to change much of our habitual pattern of thought and behaviour, and thereby learn to live more creatively.

As we develop, we will find that negative emotions caused through past experiences will begin to loosen their hold. But this will only happen if we are prepared to let go of the past and be more receptive to, and interactive with, the present. Only then can positive growth and inner healing take place, and an openness to life begin.

The story of two travelling monks coming to a stream illustrates this. A woman asks if one of them would carry her to the other side: one of them does so. A while later, the other monk can no longer keep his thoughts to himself and says, 'What a nerve the woman had to ask monks to take her across the stream!'. The other monk replies, 'Are you still carrying her? I left her by the bank of the stream.'

The story shows, simply and profoundly, how we can hold on to experiences which bind us to the past. If instead we learn to live in the present and to be open to what is happening around us, we will be able to use our experience and knowledge of life in a much more free and positive way.

If we are truly prepared to take up the challenge of knowing ourselves – physically, mentally, emotionally and spiritually – we will discover ways of bringing peace into our lives, and begin to view life from a more harmonious perspective. We will grow in wisdom and understanding, and learn how to accept and face life in all its dimensions. We will face who and what we are and what we are feeling, and truly 'be' in the present moment without holding on to the past or imposing any resistance to the things we encounter. We will be at one with ourselves, our experiences, and all of creation.

Balancing psychic and mediumistic powers with the spiritual path

We must find time to change any limiting psychological structures or behaviour. If we wish to be in harmony with the spiritual dimension of life, we must realise that the Supreme Spirit knows no boundary or prejudice. Therefore, we must also hold no set views or prejudice, but recognise that same Presence within all people, and within all that surrounds us. Finding fault in others can be more of a projection of our own minds, and shows a lack of understanding on our behalf.

We can become so entangled in the events of everyday life that we lose sight of spiritual values. Unfortunately, we have been educated to expect life to be a stream of activity – the more we do, the fuller we think our lives are. We should also guard against developing psychic and mediumistic abilities with the same attitude.

It is important not to become active to the point of developing and demonstrating these gifts only to find that we have little time for other areas of development. We must not confuse *doing* with *being*, but recognise the importance of inner development alongside any outward activity.

Placing too much emphasis on the development and practice of psychic and mediumistic abilities can lead to over-sensitivity, which becomes a problem in daily life. If their cultivation is not balanced alongside self-awareness, they will be of little value to the growth of the complete personality.

Though all these things are linked, they can function independently of one another. The development of the psychic or mediumistic faculty does not necessarily indicate spiritual growth. Truly developed individuals are identified not by any psychic or mediumistic powers they display, but by their natural goodness, compassion and wisdom.

Overcoming the things that bind

In order to develop, we will have to face and overcome any emotional blockages. We may find aspects within our nature that grate against finer qualities within us. Yet it is the grating and not the more refined that usually cries out for our attention to do something. Friction and discontent can be signs for positive growth to take place. Denying such things brings delusion and limitation, instead of growth and awareness of life in and around us. We have to learn how to accept things as they are. This means cultivating an element of flexibility and 'non-attachment', while never underestimating the positive potential each of us has.

It means facing any resistances – our deepest fears and darkest experiences – and accepting them. Through doing this, we work towards dispersing any power that we give to the things we resist. We can never become fully centred until we can do this and know what is going on beneath our surface consciousness, transforming all that appears to block our growth.

We have to be aware of our thoughts, emotions and reactions in order to discover ways to unlock and refine our spiritual potential. This is not about being self-righteous or having a cold outlook upon life. It is about living creatively, obtaining a freedom of spirit which sees and acts beyond the boundaries of limiting appearances. It is about self-growth, awakening to the good in us, and taking responsibility for our development.

If we use a simple practice like breath awareness in everyday life, it will help centre us and bring our attention back to ourselves. By becoming more aware, we become more open, giving and compassionate, as awareness also encompasses being there for others.

We should avoid any activity which stops us caring about others, and allow the spiritual Self to guide us in everything that we do. Even if we continually fail, we should realise that growth is brought about in the trying, as we often learn more from mistakes than achievements. It is also through acknowledging and accepting our imperfections that we learn humility.

When we start to transform our lives, we may notice various negatives rising to the surface. We might discover aspects about ourselves that are not pleasant. Do not be disturbed if this happens. Just accept what emerges and be positive about your growth. Noticing these things can be a sign of progression and signify that emotions that have long been denied are beginning to make themselves known. By becoming open, letting them in and owning them, you can start the healing process and work towards letting them go, and of bringing everything into line with your spiritual nature. This way your development will proceed naturally and harmoniously.

A personal realisation exercise

This exercise is a way of using the body to make you more aware of what is happening at deeper levels of your being:

1 Sit quietly with your eyes closed. Relax the body and mind, and be still and quiet for a few minutes.

2 Become conscious of your body and breathing. Mentally explore the body. Slowly go through it and see if there is anything that draws your attention.

3 Turn your awareness to anything in your body that draws you to it. Feel into it and see what it is about. Ask yourself: 'Does it feel like tension or like a knot?'; 'Does it feel like a dull ache or a sharp pain?'; 'Is it something warm or cold?'; 'Is it a comfortable or uncomfortable feeling?'.

4 Do not rush. Wait and see what comes up, and ask what it means to you: 'What is it about?'; 'What is causing it?'; 'What is it trying to tell me?'. Do not rush. Feel into your body and be aware of what is going on.

5 Return to being aware of the room you are in and write down anything that surfaced during this exercise. This will help you to keep any impressions that you had and give you something to reflect and act upon later.

Individual Development

Guiding spirits, unite us in our understanding.
Help us realise that we are all expressions of the One,
that God is ever-blissful, conscious existence.

Mistakes are sometimes made by approaching development too narrowly. We must be wary of separating different areas of development into compartments, and of having rigid ideas of how God and spirit affect and influence us, or of how we should develop.

To follow a set pattern to reach a specific goal, with little concern for the individual personality, character and deeper spiritual nature, is to assume that everyone is the same, including those in the spirit world. It shows that an open and wide view is not being taken. It is wise to investigate different areas of development in order to gain some practical knowledge, but this should lead to personal practice, experience and insight into the many different ways to God and spirit.

It is important to look at the whole of the individual, to realise that we are all different, and that our environment, emotions, experiences, abilities, family background, beliefs, achievements, pains and pleasures, will all affect our approach to development. It is from this individual viewpoint that we have to consider spiritual growth and see what it entails.

Harmonising the complete personality

Since ancient times it has been recognised that there are various conscious and unconscious qualities or levels of the individual self – higher, lower and middle (good, imperfect and moderate).[9] In order to bring about balance, we need to be aware of what is going on at every level of our being and find ways of harmonising opposing parts.

Our consciousness is usually focused only around the middle area, with perhaps occasional glimpses of the higher and lower aspects of our individual personality. Some try to deny or suppress the more negative (shadow) parts of themselves. This is a dangerous game as negativity will manifest itself in other ways. But even around the middle self, we are not always aware of what is going on.

If we become aware of our everyday activities, we will discover that we are many things: one minute the hard-nosed business person, next the loving parent, and so on. Some of the roles we play in our daily lives may be major ones, others may not. Psychotherapists often refer to these different roles as 'subpersonalities'. We may slip into a variety of them numerous times a day. Yet it is through understanding all these levels of ourselves that we develop. It is through them all that the true Self seeks to find perfect and harmonious expression – through us, in us, as us.

An instrument for the activity of the spirit

In the the development of mediumship, we have to remember that the same laws govern us all, and that the same power manifests through us all. We need to be conscious of how spirit's power affects and manifests through us, and how it will be governed by our personality and character as well as by the psychological base of our being.

Individual development will be affected by how we and the spirit work upon the potential within us. It will also be affected by our aspirations and willingness to co-operate with the spirit world, and by the spirit's ability to influence us at the various levels of our being. We should realise that only we, God and the spirit influences that surround us can develop us.

Some people have tried to standardise methods of development. This has been partly due to their feeling that because their method was right for them, it must be right for everyone. But because of our individuality, this is not so. We must never try to impose our thoughts and ideas on others, or insist that others should follow the same pattern of development that we have taken as this can only be harmful psychologically and spiritually.

It is God and the spirit working through our individuality, character and personality that should be the ground on which our development begins. We must endeavour to link with God and the spirit influences that surround us and gain guidance and direction from them. In this way, a pattern of development will establish itself in the way that God and the spirit require it to be.

We should never allow ourselves to be indoctrinated or to indoctrinate others. We should not ridicule, but encourage others and ourselves to be open, straightforward and discerning. We must develop discrimination and integrity. Through this, the influence of God and spirit will establish itself so that they and we will be of service to humanity.

*   *   *

A personal realisation exercise[10]

For the following exercise, you will need a selection of coloured crayons and some sheets of white paper approximately 420 × 300 mm (18 × 15 in):

1 Sit quietly for a few minutes with your eyes closed.

2 Ask yourself, 'What is it I want?'. Fantasise about all the things you think you desire, a new car, a dishwasher, a house in the country, a new partner, a holiday in the Greek islands, a world cruise, a wardrobe full of new clothes, etc.

3 Next, make a note of them. Choose some coloured crayons you feel attracted to and free-draw any impressions, images or feelings that you get of them. Do not worry if you cannot draw. Those without an artistic eye sometimes display more freedom in their drawing, which can be equally revealing.

4 Put your drawing aside and sit quietly again. This time ask yourself, 'What is it I need?'. This is a different question. Think about it and see what transpires.

5 Once again, make a note of anything that arises and draw any impressions, images or feelings.

6 Put the drawing aside and sit quietly. This time ask yourself, 'Is there anything that is stopping me from obtaining what I need?'. See if anything comes to mind.

7 Make a note of what arises, and draw any impressions, images or feelings.

8 Put the drawing aside and sit quietly. Now ask yourself, 'What is it that I must do to overcome my barriers?'.

9 Make a note and draw any impressions, images or feelings.

10 Place all four drawings and notes in front of you and assess your feelings about each question. Ask yourself, 'What do these drawings reveal about me and about my life?'.

Transformation

Make my heart Your loving home
and my life a true expression of the spirit.

Through knowing ourselves, we align all our actions with creative living, thought and conduct. We become centred, balanced and at one with all that we come into contact with. But a superficial interest in spiritual development will not be enough to bring about this holistic transformation. We must be dedicated and willing to learn self-mastery. This does not imply that we have to perform harsh penances. Far from it: development means awakening to a much richer, freer and fuller life.

As long as there is conflict, internal or external, in our lives, we will need to discover ways of drawing strength from our spiritual practices so that we can awaken to our spiritual consciousness.

Be aware that everything you do, say or think will inevitably affect and colour your development. Every thought and emotion has the capacity to create peace or discord, growth or restriction.

If we consider absent healing, we see that by sending out compassionate and loving thoughts we are capable of bringing about positive change. But if positive thoughts can result in healing, we must consider the influence of negative and destructive thoughts, as they can also have an effect.

Looking at ourselves in this way, we realise that we have responsibility for all that we do – a responsibility not only to ourselves, but to the whole of life around us.

Through self-awareness, we can become more conscious of the positive and negative forces within us. We can then begin to cultivate our positive potential, transform the negative and become more creative instruments for good in the world.

Letting go and letting God

Learning discipline and how to let go are two important areas of development. Through discipline we can strengthen our personal will, but not the type that makes us inflexible or dogmatic: 'for there are higher things than the ego's will, and to these one must bow'.[11]

If the personal will is developed, no longer will we be slaves to every situation that comes our way, as the will can help strengthen our commitment to the spiritual path. It can also give us the strength to let go and to 'dis-identify' ourselves from any negativity. Through letting go we can surrender and hand ourselves over to a Greater Power so that It may intervene and influence our lives and bring about positive growth. Surrender means recognising that we cannot bring about a total change in our life and our development without the aid of God or the spirit.

Both the will and the letting go are important in helping us work on the many different levels of our personalities. It is through the will that we find the strength and the courage to face any troublesome qualities within ourselves, while letting go allows us to release them, and to be freer and more open to creative growth.

Through strength of will and letting go we can all take charge of our lives and transform everything that is of no value for the road ahead. By doing so, we make room for the higher spiritual Self to influence and interact with our lives.

Swimming with the tide

There are always two ways of approaching anything: a right way and a wrong way. We can live life in a perfectly natural, open and accepting way, or impose our desires on how we wish things to be. The latter may sometimes obtain results, but it is like swimming against the tide and often leads to unwanted stress and disappointment.

If we balance our life with our spiritual nature by cultivating awareness of our thoughts, emotions and actions, and observing regular practice of prayer, contemplation and meditation, we will learn how to open ourselves, quieten the mind and see life as it is, and experience it without imposing any desire or judgement on it or putting up resistance to it. We will see things as they are, and overcome any boundaries between us and others. With this new-found insight, we will not only understand life and ourselves better, but also start to understand and feel more for others. This is the true meaning of compassion.

Acceptance does not mean that we become inactive or passive. If properly used, acceptance becomes a creative act, which leads to spiritual growth in a natural way. It is an integral part of the growing process. Through it we learn to live and act in harmony with all and take responsibility for all areas of our lives.

When we allow the True Self to surface and to influence our lives, we will discover ways to become more balanced, caring and 'nonattached' (flexible without holding on to any experiences). If we give ourselves to this life, we shall embrace the God in all, and find that in return our lives are enriched by being embraced by God.

Handling experiences on the path

Travelling a spiritual path is not about seeking experiences, but unfolding our spiritual nature and letting it have more influence on us.

Nonetheless, experiences of various kinds can happen. They may occur slowly and gradually. There may be periods of sudden experience, then nothing for months. At these times, things may be occurring at deeper levels than we are aware of. Periods of spiritual dryness, such as the dark night of the soul can sometimes happen. But by going through the experience we will discover new strength.

Do not hang on to any experience that you may have as this can block future progress. Do not let your ego get the better of you by believing that a particular experience makes you different from anyone else. Instead, let the influence of any experience open you and expand your awareness of life. Let it influence you in a positive way.

Awakening to inner light

By awakening to the spiritual dimension of life, we have the capacity to become more centred and loving. Instead of being pulled in all directions and allowing ourselves to be swayed by ingrained thoughts and emotions, we can open ourselves to joy and freedom, and experience life in a peaceful and balanced frame of mind.

Through creative self-development we become aware of the spirit that we are, and realise that nothing of this world is permanent, except the indestructible part of God that works through all.

Let the appearance of anything that separates you from recognising this dissolve. Allow this to open you to greater things. The tangible, living presence of God and the spirit will come easily to those who are pure and compassionate in their hearts, and open in their thoughts.

*　　*　　*

A personal realisation

I am one with the Infinite, Loving Spirit. I release all discord and negativity from my life. I am a true representative of the Infinite Good, practising non-injury in thought, word and deed and realising that all is equal in the eyes of the Supreme Spirit. I have control over the judging mind. I am selfless in my actions — truthful and open to myself and others — following God and the spirit's direction, not mine, making every action for the growth of spiritual awareness and the realisation of the inner Self.

Openness

Seeing into the nature of all things,
I awaken to a life of truth and openness.

Life is about growth, starting from small beginnings and evolving into maturity. All life needs the right kind of nourishment in order to grow healthily. All around us, life can be seen in an infinite variety of manifestations – it is both creative and expressive. We should realise that we too are part of this life and part of nature. Just as everything in nature requires food for growth, so do travellers on the spiritual path.

Nourishment can come from prayer, meditation and contemplation, or from lectures, reading and speaking to those with insight into the spiritual life. Yet merely reading or listening to others speaking about development will not by itself awaken or increase our spiritual awareness, for the spiritual life has to be lived. Knowledge can be invaluable, but life is the ultimate training ground.

Theoretical knowledge that serves no purpose other than to stimulate the intellect will not by itself help us develop: in some circumstances it can interfere with development. For knowledge to have positive use, it must have a 'transformative function', something that leads us to fuller expression and growth, and to a greater understanding of ourselves and others. It should help us overcome all sense of separation from the vast ocean of life around us, and truly live the universal life.

The universality of the Spirit

If we study the lives of those who have travelled the universal path before us – individuals who have lived the spiritual life to the full – we can learn and be inspired by them. We can discover the practices they found helpful, and truths they may have discovered. If we allow their words to take root in our consciousness, their insight can inspire us in our development, and help us to understand what living a truly spiritual life entails. On the surface we may find contradictions to what we and others believe in. But it should be remembered that each of us will see things from our own individual standpoint.

The following story, about three blind men who try to describe an elephant, can be found in many cultures. One of them feels one of the elephant's ears and says, 'It is large and like a rug'. Another feels a leg and says, 'It is round and firm like a pillar'. The third feels the elephant's trunk and says, 'It is long and like a pipe'.[12] Their descriptions are not wrong, but they do not describe the complete reality.

Diverse as teachings of the spiritual life may seem, there are always threads of truth to be found. When we examine people's search for the spiritual dimension of life, we are looking at their struggle to find the truth within – describing their findings in whatever words they can bring to mind to express the inexpressible. In understanding the teachings of the world, we come to appreciate the many different cultures of the world, and the various ways in which we can grow and realise our true nature.

Too often we limit development. Concepts are often built around experiences and lose much of what the experience was about. To believe that only one tradition or type of development has all the answers, and has discovered all there is to know about God, spirit, the human mind, or the Ultimate Reality that lies behind all forms, is clearly a display of spiritual pride and of prejudice towards others, and can only cause division instead of harmony.

The one quest

If we wish to discover a greater truth, then we must be prepared to let go of restrictive ideas about life, spirit and ways in which we can develop. Those whose spiritual eye is open will put differences aside and see the Supreme Spirit at work through everything. Yet the spiritual life will often challenge the accepted standard of thinking, and can sometimes trigger a negative response in those who are not open to development. We are, after all, creatures of habit, and do not like our world being turned upside-down. But we should never force views on anyone, especially those who are not ready to accept the challenge of change. Let us instead encourage ourselves and others who are searching to be more open, centred and compassionate, and make our lives the example by which we are measured.

We should always be moving towards wider possibilities of development. It isn't always enough that knowledge is handed down from one to another. We still need to find, experience and learn for ourselves. Truth must always be sought by the individual as it has been in every age.

Spiritual evolution

To develop ourselves, we must be willing to progress and to be open to new knowledge and new experience. If we are set in our views, we are in danger of stagnation and of stifling the spirit that we are. Through the cultivation of open minds and hearts, we can connect more with ourselves and others, be in tune with all things, and cease limiting ourselves to restrictive concepts or emotions which may create barriers to development.

We should realise that our reason for searching is that we do not have all the answers. We should let new knowledge and experience open us to newer fields of vision. For if we are truly prepared to develop, what we may think of as fact today may look different to us tomorrow. This is not to say that what we have so far discovered and believe to be true is false, any more than a view from a mountain's peak makes what is seen from the ground incorrect. It means that we should allow ourselves to see life from a wider perspective. In obtaining this new outlook, we will find all areas of our lives evolving in a more harmonious and natural way.

Seeing beyond limitations, we find truth in all things. Although our bodies appear to be made from physical matter, our essence is spirit. It is the realisation of the spirit that we have to develop and allow to shine through in this life.

Underlying all teachings there is one Reality, one Ultimate Truth, manifesting in an infinite variety of ways. Some call it 'God' or 'Spirit'. Others say It can only be referred to in negative terms (what It is not) because It is beyond all words and concepts, and cannot be understood until It has been personally realised. To this Reality we owe our very existence. In order to become more receptive instruments through which It may express Itself, we have to relinquish all narrowness of vision, recognise the good within us, and allow our true nature to manifest itself more fully in this world.

*   *   *

A personal realisation

I treat all people equally, and embrace a life of freedom, truth and openness.

Exercises:
A Daily Programme

Lead me forever onwards to Your understanding.

The exercises in this chapter are simple practices that can be incorporated into your daily life. They are designed to help you become more conscious of your thoughts and emotions, and make you more positively aware of your actions. One or two practices have been mentioned briefly elsewhere, but what we hope to do in this chapter is suggest ways in which you can implement them in your life.

Unless you suffer from a particular health problem, you should not find difficulty with anything that follows. If you do, then ask yourself why. Is it because there is something that you are not facing and accepting within yourself? Remember that resistance can often be felt before a door is opened.

To the following exercises could be added others, such as chanting mantras or incorporating an element of ritual. You must discover what is best suited to your nature and lifestyle, and seek out practices that will be of use to you. You are in charge of your own development.

Having a regular programme can help establish a solid base from which we can draw strength and guidance in our lives. Try to practise at a regular time. You will be less likely to miss your practices if you make them part of your daily routine. Give yourself plenty of time to do any of the following exercises. Do not rush them. Your attitude to the whole day starts here.

1. Upon awakening

As soon as you wake, gather your thoughts and become aware of your entire body. Feel its weight upon the bed. Mentally become alive and visualise energy and life going into every part of your body, into every muscle, joint and cell. Gently tense and release your muscles, and stretch your limbs. Become conscious of yourself, aware of the precious gift of life running through you.

Arise slowly and consciously. Stand up and inhale fully through your nostrils while raising your arms forward to shoulder level. Hold your breath for three to five seconds, according to your lung capacity. Breathe out, lowering your arms to your sides, and let go of all tension. Sense peace and calm entering your body and mind. Allow them to permeate the room and your environment – even if you live in a noisy city.

2. Prayer

Gather your thoughts, focus your mind upon the Supreme Spirit and voice a simple prayer. Do not do this glibly; put real feeling behind the words.

Example:

> *Gracious Spirit, guide me through the coming day*
> *and help me to establish Your light and love within.*

3. Preparing yourself

As you perform your morning ablutions, observe your actions and the sensation of water touching your body. Feel it bringing life and vitality to your skin and body. Water is a vital substance of life, and is considered sacred in many spiritual traditions. Indeed it is; life cannot survive long on earth without it.

Bathing is important, not only because it has a soothing effect upon the body, but also because it soothes and refreshes the mind. It opens the pores and allows toxins to escape, and so helps us to become more healthy.

Sip a cup of hot, boiled water on an empty stomach every morning. This encourages good action of the digestive system and is a natural remedy for purifying internal organs.

As you prepare yourself for the coming day, be aware of your actions and thoughts. Whether you are brushing your teeth, preparing the children for school, getting dressed, or combing your hair, do it mindfully and in a tranquil frame of mind.

4. Physical exercise

Because your body is the temple in which your spirit resides, it is a good idea to start the day with some form of physical exercise. This will help keep your body supple and free from tension, and your mind more focused. Exercises are not just for the physical body, but also have a spiritual purpose. To help you be more aware of this, you can use affirmations with your practices such as, 'I have strength and life in my whole being'; 'I am centred in awareness'; 'God's peace flows through me, in me, now'.

Some may wish to practise hatha yoga at this point, whilst others may prefer something less demanding. Simple exercises for loosening up the neck and shoulders will stop tension building up in these areas. Briskly patting the whole of the body, face, arms and legs with the palms of your hands has a marvellous energising effect.

Whatever you decide, do it gently and rhythmically, putting life and energy into your body. But note that any form of strenuous physical exercise should be performed on an empty stomach. Wait for at least three hours after your last meal, and half an hour following a drink.

We would recommend that anyone who wishes to know more about yoga exercises should consult a qualified teacher and get expert tuition before practising on their own. Do not try to learn yoga from books or videos as you can easily strain or damage yourself if you practise wrongly.

5. A short reading

Spend a few moments each morning reading a short passage from a spiritually uplifting book. This will help bring the mind to a more responsive state for meditation later on, and uplift and encourage you in your practice.

6. Relaxing and breathing exercise

Remember that breathing is the most vital force of energy. It is a form of nutrition, just as food is. The following relaxation and breathing exercise will help relax the mind and body, and put you in a more responsive state for meditating.

1   Sit in a quiet place, where you will not be disturbed. Sit or kneel with your eyes closed in your preferred meditation position, keeping your spine erect.

2   Mentally check for any tension in your body, starting with your feet and slowly working your way up to the top of your head. Be aware of any tension being held in parts of your body, paying particular attention to your neck, shoulder and facial areas. As you go from one area to another, mentally say to yourself, 'My ... (name the part) is free from tension and relaxed.' Release any tension with the out-breath.

Once you have completed this exercise, mentally tell yourself, 'My whole body is now free from all tension and is totally relaxed'. This whole exercise should take approximately five to ten minutes to do each morning.

3   Bring your awareness to your breathing. Exhale through both nostrils, gently pulling in on the lower abdominal muscles at the end of the exhalation. Using your right hand, place your thumb at the side of your right nostril and stop the flow of air through the nostril. Do not use use too much pressure. Gently breathe in through your left nostril to the count of three or five, whatever is most comfortable. Then gently breathe out through your left nostril to the count of three or five. Do this five times.

Place the third (ring) finger at the side of your left nostril and stop the flow of air through it. Gently breathe in through your right nostril to the count of three or five. Then gently breathe out through your right nostril to the count of three or five. Do this five times.

Keep your awareness on your breathing, and gently inhale through both nostrils to the count of three or five. Then gently exhale through both nostrils to the count of three or five, carefully pulling in on the lower abdominal muscles at the end of each exhalation. Do this five times.

At the end of the practice, sit quietly for a moment and mentally say to yourself, 'Peace, love, harmony and goodness'.

If you do these exercises each morning, they will help keep your nasal passages clear and your mind refreshed and alert. Retention of the in-breath can be introduced to the last breathing exercise to the count of three or five, but only if it feels comfortable. Do not strain or force your breathing. Stop the practice if any discomfort is felt.

7. Using sound to evoke body awareness and focus the mind

Sit in your chosen meditation position with your spine erect. Close your eyes and slowly inhale a deep breath. Then gently close your ears with your index fingers (do not apply too much pressure) and make a gentle humming sound as you exhale. Repeat three to five times. As you do this, be aware of the sound vibrating within your body and the air around you. This exercise can help relax and focus the mind before meditating, and help energise the body and mind.

8. Meditation

This example of meditation can help to bring the whole of you into balance: body, mind, emotions and spirit. It should take approximately 20 to 30 minutes to practise each morning. It can be lengthened slightly by first envisaging a deeper shade of the following colours, then perceiving a lighter pastel shade.

Relax and breathe normally, slowly and rhythmically. Then breathe in the following colours. Do not rush from one colour to another, but spend time with each. Note the change in vibration of each. Feel it permeate the whole of your being.

1   Imagine and breathe in the colour red. See this colour as being quite bright and luminous, and slowly sense it coming up from the ground. Feel it entering into your body, balancing and spiritualising all organs, making every part of you function optimally, in harmony with itself. Feel it energising your entire being.

2   See this red change slowly into a vibrant shade of orange, coming up from the earth and bringing vitality and health to your body.

3   Next, picture a bright yellow coming up. Feel a clearness of mind and a relaxing of your body.

4   See this shade of yellow change slowly into a rich, luminous green coming horizontally all around you. Within it, feel the natural vibration of nature. Feel at one and in harmony with all life.

5 Now picture and inhale a bright luminous blue coming from above. Feel its calming, peaceful influence upon you. Know that this colour is restoring health and balance to your body, mind and emotions.

6 Next, picture a vibrant pastel shade of indigo descending all around you. Feel this colour awakening your inner spirit, harmonising all the other parts of your being. Sense it enveloping you and lifting your consciousness to God.

7 Let this colour slowly change into a pastel shade of violet, and feel it permeating everything around you. Feel this colour coming down above your head, just out of your field of vision, pouring over the whole of your being. Breathe this colour in and know that within it you may find time to rest and soothe your body, mind and spirit in the loving presence of God. Know that this colour will restore and replenish your whole Self. Breathe in this presence: feel it all around you. Feel all that is good in life – peace, love, joy, light and beauty. Know that you are a pure manifestation of God; that God does not work against Itself, but seeks to be whole and perfect. Seek to find this perfect Self and let It shine through and permeate your entire being. Stay with this feeling for a while and strengthen your contact with God.

8 Slowly become aware of your surroundings and collect your thoughts. Finish with a positive affirmation:

> *Today I awaken to God in all things. I acknowledge God's power working in me, through me and around me. I am aware that my spirit within is perfect, and I let this perfect spirit of goodness permeate my whole being, bringing all of my life into harmony.*

9. Awareness

Do not dissipate the work you have performed on yourself in chatter. Cultivate peace, and have control over your thoughts. As you prepare and eat breakfast and other meals, be aware of what you are doing. Whenever possible, eat in silence. Be aware of external sounds as well as your own inner thoughts and emotions, but do this with an element of 'nonattachment'. Build on the peace and strength you have found. Understand that it is not just the material substance of food that gives you energy: the thought you put behind it energises it. Be thankful for it, know that it has grown on God's earth, and that God's creative energy is contained within it.

10. A guide to the day

Throughout the rest of the day, make a conscious effort to re-establish your contact with God. Be conscious of your thoughts and actions. Find time to be quiet in mind and body for a few minutes at different times of the day. Whenever possible, bring your attention back to your breathing and make a conscious effort to centre your thoughts and emotions.

Living creatively means working towards a greater awareness of life, becoming more in harmony with life around us, and anchoring ourselves more firmly in God's presence.

If at all possible, walk in the fresh air. Walk where there are trees, where there is nature – in a park or forest. Look for God's presence in the growth of life around you. Realise that everything is alive in God and saturated in Its Divinity – that you are part of that Divinity and part of nature. As you do so, take a deep breath and feel your whole self being energised and harmonised by the vast ocean of life around you.

Take a spiritually uplifting book with you. Sit and read a passage or two. Then be still and quiet for a moment and know that all is well in God's presence.

Use keywords such as 'peace', 'joy', 'love', 'acceptance', 'trust', 'let go', or a positive affirmation at different times in the day to help you keep that link with the spiritual side of nature. Say them frequently to yourself and feel their influence upon your consciousness. Choose your words carefully. What you feed into your consciousness will be reflected in your life. The mind draws towards itself the things with which it is in tune. Everything responds to you at your current level of understanding and awareness. For this reason we should watch our thoughts, emotions and actions throughout the day and cultivate creative thinking, conduct and speech.

11. A guide to problems

If you encounter a problem, this exercise may help you to see it from a different angle:

First, find time to be quiet, calm and still for a few moments. Check that your breathing is calm, rhythmic and relaxed. If it is not, practise the relaxation and breathing exercise mentioned earlier in this chapter and feel yourself becoming more peaceful. Now use the following affirmation, taking its full meaning into your consciousness:

Knowing that Spirit is the One Power that governs all and that this Perfect Power flows through me, I know of no limitation in my life and claim a life of infinite possibilities. I am a non-resistant instrument for truth, love and goodness.

As the Infinite Spirit within me knows no boundaries, there is nothing that I cannot do, face or overcome. All is in harmony with my life. I am at peace with all that surrounds me. I see through all things and recognise the Divine Presence in the centre of all.

Do not at any time make affirmative statements about the particular problem you are facing. To do otherwise would mean underrating the power of the Supreme Spirit and give power to any problem you face. This does not mean that we should not explore our pains, fears and emotions; we should discover ways to understand them, own them and transform them.

12. A guide to the evening

Find time in the evening to be quiet and reflect upon your day. Look for any negative areas that need more attention. Ask yourself whether there is anything within you that you need to be more aware of. Is there anything on which you need to work or change? Is there something you need at this moment in time? Make a note and keep a journal of any thoughts. Be honest with yourself and use your journal to help you understand and know the way you work – physically, mentally, emotionally and spiritually.

Round off your day by reading a passage from a spiritually sound and uplifting book. Follow it with the relaxation and breathing exercise and a period of prayer and meditation (see the chapters on these for guidance).

Finish by sending out some healing thoughts to those whom you know need help, and to the leaders of all nations to make peace with one another, to the animal and plant kingdom, and to the world at large. Distant healing has a positive effect not only on those to whom you direct it, but also upon yourself. It helps strengthen your spiritual nature – your feelings of love, peace, unity and compassion.

When you retire for the night, thank God for your life and for all the good in your life.

The exercises suggested in this chapter and book will hopefully give readers some guidance on centring their lives in the spirit. We do not wish readers to follow everything without question, but would prefer them to take on board only that which feels right for their development. We hope readers will continue to search for and discover ways of tapping into and unfolding their spiritual nature.

May the path you tread be blessed with love and wisdom and be full of eternal joy and peace.

Notes

1. Quote from John I:I, *Holy Bible: New International Version*, Hodder and Stoughton, 1988 reprint, page 148.

2. Based around a meditation practice by Swami Shivapremananda, *A Guide to Meditation: Part 2, Yoga and Health Magazine*, April 1995, pages 29–31.

3. 'The popular opinion that these yogic abilities are not part of the path to Self-realisation is demonstrably wrong … they *cannot* be separated from the essentially organic and unitary structure of Yoga.' George Feuerstein, *The Yoga-Sutras of Patanjali*, Inner Traditions International, 1989 reprint, pages 104–5.

4. A view expressed by C.G. Jung (also shared by William James), in James Fadiman and Robert Frager, *Personality and Personal Growth*, HarperCollins, 1994, 3rd edition, page 86.

5. Information about Thomas Young and the Trichromacy Theory are from *The Guinness Encyclopedia of the Living World* Guinness Publishing, 1992, page 189.

6. Paragraph based on H.L. Cooke, *Painting Techniques of the Masters*, Watson Guptil, 1972, page 38.

7. H.L. Cooke, *Painting Techniques of the Masters*, Watson Guptil, 1972, page 39.

8. D. McMonagle, *Science: Basic Facts*, HarperCollins, 1992, pages 51–2.

9. Ancient yogic text mentions the three *gunas*. The Swiss psychiatrist, Carl Jung, wrote much on coming to terms with the shadow side of the personality and balancing it with the light. Roberto Assagioli formulated ideas around three levels of self.

10. Based around a combination of exercises used in psychosynthesis workshops.

11. C.G. Jung, *Memories, Dreams, Reflections*, Fontana Press, 1983, page 205.

12. Robert E. Ornstein, *The Psychology of Consciousness*, Jonathan Cape, 1975, page 145.

Appendix I

Dynamic Thought
by Glyn Edwards

Thought is a dynamic, living force. Some regard it as the most vital, subtle and irresistible force that exists in the universe. Much of what we see and know as real in the physical dimension of life is a creation of thought. For instance, buildings are the products of the thoughts of architects, cars of designers and engineers, medicine of biochemists, and art of artists.

The thought world is more real – relatively – than the physical universe because thoughts are actual living things. Every change in our thought will resonate with the vibration of its matter, which is mental. For thought, as a force, needs a certain kind of subtle matter in its workings.

Our thoughts will take on the form of anything they contemplate. For example, when we think of an object, our mind shapes itself into the form of that object. This is how we perceive, not just through sight or touch, but through the mind. It is the mind that directs the other senses and affects the auric field. When we change our thoughts, our mind also alters its shape. If we observe some of the processes of our mind and thoughts we will notice many modifications continually arising in the mind. As our thoughts change, so does our mind. So, therefore, does our auric field.

We need to understand the value and practice of prayer, meditation and silence in order that we can steady, fix and empower our thought. This will affect and change certain energies within our body, mind and auric field, and bring about balance in the various levels of that energy. This attracts the right things, spiritually as well as physically, into our life and development.

Because the aura is affected by our thoughts, we should realise that they will play a dominant role in our development. Some mediums are able to see the effects that different thoughts have on the aura, and the various potentials that a person may have.

Though thought may be described as subtle matter, it is in many ways as solid as stone. For though the physical frame may die, our thoughts go on resonating in the ether. Because thought, like our spirit, never dies.

We should, in our spiritual development, work upon our thought so that we can develop right thinking. Remember the saying, 'As a man thinks, so he becomes'. Whatever you focus your mind upon will become part of your character. Realise that your thoughts will mould and shape not only your character, but also your auric energy at every level of your being. Thoughts from an outside source can and do have an impact on the aura. We encounter this external influence almost every day, in all areas of our lives: in our environment, the people we meet, and activities we undertake. All these affect and colour our thoughts.

We translate thought impressions continuously into our current way of thinking. These find expression in our mind and aura. This is why it is important to choose our friends carefully, especially on the spiritual level.

We have the power to change and grow

If you think you are weak, then weak you will be. If you believe you cannot do something, then you will probably not be able to. We all form our characters by becoming what we think whilst our characters recreate the world in which we live. Everything we see, feel, hear and touch is an expression of our thoughts. This can be understood by observing the shifts in our different moods. When we are happy, the world becomes a beautiful place; when we are sad, it is not. This does not mean that we each cannot change our character and perception of life, because we can, by reprogramming our thoughts. It is we who place the limitations upon ourselves.

In development, as the influence of the spirit becomes more effective, their thoughts will co-mingle with ours. Yet it is still our choice to what extent we allow the spirit's influence to affect us. We see from this how important it is to know our thoughts as through them we will attract corresponding influences. As we attract, so do we repel. This law of attraction and repulsion can be seen operating on both the spiritual and physical levels of being.

Focusing the mind

Most of our thoughts are not well grounded. Often, the images of our thoughts are not clear, strong or well defined. But through reflection and meditation we can clarify our thoughts. This will encourage them to settle down and to crystallise into definite shape.

Through right thinking, reasoning, introspection and meditation we can enhance our thoughts and ideas. With this process we start to gain more control over our thoughts, which should be an integral part of development. By having control over our thoughts we can become aware of the level of consciousness we are using at any given time.

We also need to know how to apply our thinking and sustain a positive attitude to life. Applied thinking focuses the mind on an object of thought. Sustained positive thought keeps the mind continually engaged in the act of creating, bringing attitudes towards ourselves, others and our environment. This enables us to perceive through the intuitive level of our minds, discover the right directions to take in life, and focus our talents and potentials. It helps us to create a new environment in our own minds, which enables us to receive and create thoughts that are inspiring and infused from a level beyond ourselves.

The power of the mind

We need to understand how, by bringing the full weight and power of the mind behind prayer and meditation, we can enable them to become effective and creative tools in our development.

We must realise that everything we do begins in the mind, and that for us to bring our minds to exert their full power, we need to focus the power of our thought.

In our spiritual development we aim to bring about some movement in our consciousness so that we can comprehend what lies beyond the senses of sight, hearing, touch, taste and smell. This may happen spontaneously. Yet to develop our potential, we need to apply something more. We have to focus our minds and thoughts in order to inspire sustained spontaneous awareness. By focusing our minds and thoughts we can bring this about.

Internalising awareness

We need to learn how to develop the concentrative powers of the mind so that when we meditate, or when communication with the spirit world is taking place, we are able to focus our whole awareness upon what we are doing.

We need to learn how to gather our thoughts and steady them. The greatest impediment to this form of concentration is restlessness and distraction. Much has been written about concentration, yet if we observe our minds and thoughts, we will see that they have a natural tendency to wander. Often there is a never-ending stream of connected and disconnected thoughts. Our minds also experience periods of dullness, forgetfulness and laziness.

Although we all have some ability to concentrate – without it we would be unable to complete any task – full concentration can only be achieved when we are totally relaxed mentally, physically and emotionally. For many, concentration is impossible to achieve for any length of time, and trying to force the mind to concentrate can mean suppressing much of what is going on at various levels of our personalities. This is why it is important to understand and know ourselves, to learn about our thoughts, emotions and body. This is also why relaxation exercises before meditation are so important. If we cannot relax, we will not be able to meditate, or in the case of mediumship, properly attune to the spirit world.

For spiritual development, our concentration needs to be developed to a higher degree. If we have an appreciable degree of concentration, we will be able to do more and achieve more. To make spiritual progress we have to go beyond ordinary concentration, to the level where mind and consciousness are brought into tune and influenced by their spiritual aspect in order to bring about changes in the whole process of our being, both physically and spiritually.

But for many of us, our minds are only occasionally steady and truly focused. In spiritual and psychic development, we are dealing with energies that are constantly fluctuating, and display subtleties that our normal state of mind misses or misinterprets. So we need to learn how to interpret and watch the mind carefully. We do this by becoming an inner spectator, sitting and watching the mind go through its mental activities, as though we were watching a film.

As the mind begins to realise that we are not becoming involved with our thoughts, it starts to settle. It is at this point that we can introduce a word, attribute, or spiritual concept, and allow our attention and awareness to flow towards that.

If thoughts intrude, we should not become disturbed or involved in them, but allow them to come and go and return to the object of our attention. We simply watch our thoughts and let them go, without trying to suppress them, or becoming anxious about them.

If emotions intrude, follow the same principle: simply watch them come and go. They will soon pass. But do not attempt to drive them away, for you will cause mental strain and disturbance.

A time will come when through this practice you will stay for longer in uninterrupted attention and be well on your way to developing true concentration. But go gently and do not exert force. Remember to avoid tension anywhere in the body or mind.

Appendix II

Reflections from a Spiritual Notebook
by Santoshan
First published in the *Dharma Journal*

Vivekananda said we can never 'know' God, as knowing implies using the intellect, which is limited, and what we perceive around us we modify. We can only absorb so much detail at a time and never take in the 'whole'. It is rather like the drawing one often sees in psychology books where two faces of women are drawn, one old and one young. We only see one face or the other, never the two together.

It is at times when we simply allow ourselves to be that there is a widening of our consciousness and our spiritual nature is more fully realised.

*   *   *

Those who seek the path to God have to be prepared to face the fire of purification. God shapes and bends the metal of our being towards It in order to make us in the image that It has designed for us. Instead of kicking against the trials that God places before us, we should be thankful that God considers us strong enough, and has chosen us for whatever purpose.

*   *   *

It does not matter how we turn to God. If our motives are pure God will meet us halfway. We do not pray, but God prays in us. It is, in fact, a way of unknowing, as well as knowing, that leads us to resting in God's presence. It is a creative and an active path, not one of quiet inactivity.

*   *   *

We are often drawn into a deep silence which does not judge, yet emphasises many of our rough edges. All we can do is offer them up to God, for God has far more wisdom in knowing how to deal with them than we do.

*   *   *

What follows is a guide to the right use of affirmations. It does not mean that we should not use affirmations to help us develop and recognise the spirit within, but that affirmations should, as mentioned in the Word Power chapter of this book, be used alongside acceptance. Although positive thought can play an important part in development, it is not the whole of development. If unchecked, it can lead to the ego's glorification.

If on the other hand we look at Buddhists – who accept suffering as part of the human condition, rather than denying it, as some would advocate – we do not find them falling ill because they have accepted a negative condition. Instead, they use practices which help them see life as it is. In actual fact, it is a positive path. By seeing things as they are, we do not delude ourselves, but become aware of life and of truly experiencing it.

If we undertake positive affirmations in our spiritual development, we must check that they are being used to awaken us to life, to our finer qualities, and to God's power and influence, not as an escape from what may be confronting us.

It can take time for cogs to turn and for matters to fall into place. Quite often events will happen when we stop trying to enforce our will and let God take over for a change. If we are affirming all kinds of statements for circumstances to be different from what they are, we could easily be wasting our energy. Even if we get what we are asking for, it may well be the very thing that stops us from fulfiling our true destinies.

Vocal prayer is often seen as inferior, yet if used correctly, it can move mountains because it leaves things in the hands of God instead of trying to influence events that favour us over others. By simply saying, 'Here I am, show me how I may best serve You and do Your work and will', we will find ourselves guided on to a path of humility, without the threat of ego getting in the way.

By attempting to change the reality of events, we may be trying to bring something about that is not actually possible or right for us. We should instead learn to live more fully in the present and not in some wish-fulfilling fantasy. Instead of seeking to deny or remove through affirmation something that we do not want to face, we should learn how best to deal with it. The present is the only true thing that happens to us – everything else is either past memories or thoughts that may or may not come into being.

*　　*　　*

We may have all kinds of mystical experiences while travelling the spiritual path, and these can often be by-products of development. Although they can be significant at the time they occur, we should avoid being attached to any experience we may have, and remember that the aim of spiritual growth is to increase our spiritual awareness and be more selfless and compassionate human beings.

Recommended Reading

Titles marked with an asterisk* are highly recommended.

Psychical Research and the Hidden Potential in Humankind

Paul Beard, *Survival of Death*, Pilgrim Books.

Nona Coxhead, *Mind Power*, Mandala.

Brian Inglis, *Science and Parascience: A History of the Paranormal, 1914–1939*, Hodder & Stoughton (out of print).

Raynor C. Johnson, *The Imprisoned Splendour*, Hodder & Stoughton.

David Lorimer, *Whole in One: The Near Death Experience and the Ethic of Interconnectedness*, Arkana.

Archie Roy, *The Archives of the Mind*, SNU Publications.

Mediumship

Silver Birch, *Spirit Speaks*, Psychic Press.

Harry Boddington, *Materialisations*, Psychic Press.

Harry Boddington, *University of Spiritualism*, Psychic Press (out of print).

Harry Edwards, *A Guide to the Development of Mediumship*, Psychic Press.

Arthur Findlay, *On the Edge of the Etheric*, SNU Publications.

J.J. Morse, *Practical Occultism*, Psychic Press (out of print).

Ursula Roberts, *All About Mediumship*, Two Worlds.

Transpersonal Psychology and Studies in Spiritual Consciousness

Roberto Assagioli, *Psychosynthesis*, Aquarian.

Michael J. Eastcott, *'I', the Story of the Self*, Rider.

* Vivianne Crowley, *Jungian Spirituality*, Thorsons.

* James Fadiman and Robert Frager, *Personality and Personal Growth* (3rd edition), HarperCollins (out of print).

* Piero Ferrucci, *What We May Be*, Aquarian.

* William James, *The Varieties of Religious Experience*, Fount Paperbacks.

Dalai Lama, Benson, Thurman, Gardner and Goleman, *Mind Science: An East–West Dialogue*, Wisdom.

Methods of Meditation

Achaan Chah, *A Still Forest Pool*, Quest Books.
Roy Eugene Davis, *An Easy Guide to Meditation*, CSA Press.
Eknath Easwaran, *Meditation*, Nilgiri.
Jack Kornfield, *A Path with Heart*, Rider.
Thich Nhat Hanh, *The Miracle of Mindfulness*, Rider.
Stephen Levine, *A Gradual Awakening*, Gateway.
Kathleen McDonald, *How to Meditate*, Wisdom.
Venerable Henepola Gunaratana, *Mindfulness in Plain English*, Wisdom.
Venerable Mengola, *The Practice of Recollection*, The Buddhist Society.
* John Novak, *How to Meditate*, Crystal Clarity.
Monks of the Ramakrishna Order, *Meditation*, Ramakrishna Vedanta Centre.
Hari Prasad Shastri, *Meditation: Its Theory and Practice*, Shanti Sadan.

Methods of Prayer

* Eric Butterworth, *The Universe is Calling*, Harper San Francisco.
M.V. Dunlop, *Contemplative Meditation*, Fellowship of Meditation.
* Frances W. Foulks, *Effectual Prayer*, Unity Books.
Shirley C. Hughson, *Contemplative Prayer*, SPCK (out of print).
Thomas Keating, *Open Mind, Open Heart*, Element.

Mantra

Swami Vishnu Devananda, *Meditation and Mantras*, Om Lotus.
Eknath Easwaran, *The Unstruck Bell*, Nilgiri.
* Pandit Rajmani Tigunait, *The Power of Mantra and the Mystery of Initiation*, Yoga International Books.
Swami Sivananda Radha, *Mantras: Words of Power*, Timeless Books.

Health and Nutrition

H. Winter Griffith, *Complete Guide to Vitamins, Minerals and Supplements*, Fisher Books.
Alix Kirsta, *The Book of Stress Survival*, Thorsons.
Linus Pauling, *How to Live Long and Feel Better*, Avon Books.

Exercises for Health, Vitality and Spiritual Development

Omraam Mikhaël Aïvanhov, *A New Earth*, Editions Prosveta.
Master Lam Kam Chuen, *The Way of Energy*, Gaia Books.

* Swami Dharmānanda Saraswati, *Breath of Life*, Dharma Yoga Centre.
Swami Satyananda Saraswati, *Sure Ways to Self-Realization*, Bihar School of Yoga.

Retreat Guides
Roger Housden, *Retreat: Time Apart for Silence and Solitude*, Thorsons.
Stafford Whiteaker, *The Good Retreat Guide*, Rider.

Facing and Overcoming Illness and Caring for the Dying
* Julie Friedeberger, *A Visible Wound: A Healing Journey through Breast Cancer*, Element.
Elisabeth Kübler-Ross, *On Death and Dying*, Collier.
Stephen Levine, *Who Dies?*, Doubleday.
Sogyal Rinpoche, *The Tibetan Book of Living and Dying*, Rider.

New Thought and Personal Development
Ronald Beesley, *Service to the Race*, Neville Spearman.
Raymond Charles Barker, *You Are Invisible*, DeVorss.
Roy Eugene Davis, *Studies in Truth*, CSA Press.
* Emmet Fox, *The Sermon on the Mount*, HarperCollins.
Joel S. Goldsmith, *A Parenthesis in Eternity*, HarperCollins.
Joel S. Goldsmith, *Practising the Presence*, Fowler.
Ernest Holmes, *The Science of Mind*, Putnam.
Ernest Holmes, *This Thing Called You*, Putnam.
Ursula Roberts, *Hints on Spiritual Unfoldment*, Psychic Press.
* Ralph Waldo Trine, *In Tune with the Infinite*, Mandala.

The Yogic Tradition
Georg Feuerstein, *Textbook of Yoga*, Rider (out of print).
Gopi Krishna, *Higher Consciousness*, Julian Press.
M.P. Pandit, *The Yoga of Love*, Lotus Light Publications.
Ramacharaka, *Fourteen Lessons in Yogi Philosophy and Oriental Occultism*, Fowler.
Swami Paramananda, *Faith as a Constructive Force*, Vedanta Centre.
Vivekananda, *The Yogas and Other Works*, Ramakrishna-Vivekananda Centre.
Paramahansa Yogananda, *Man's Eternal Quest*, Self-realisation Fellowship.

The Buddhist Tradition

Thich Nhat Hanh, *The Heart of the Buddha's Teachings*, Parallax Press.

Ayya Khema, *Being Nobody, Going Nowhere*, Wisdom.

Myokyo-Ni, *Gentling the Bull: The Ten Bull Pictures*, The Zen Centre.

Walpola Rahula, *What the Buddha Taught*, Oneworld.

Gesha Rabten and Geshe Dhargyey, *Advice from a Spiritual Friend*, Wisdom.

Sharon Salzberg, *Loving-Kindness*, Shambhala.

Shunryu Suzuki, *Zen Mind, Beginner's Mind*, Weatherhill.

Tarthang Tulku, *Gestures of Balance*, Dharma Publishing.

Tarthang Tulku, *Openness Mind*, Dharma Publishing.

Modern Sufi Writers in the West

Reshad Feild, *The Alchemy of the Heart*, Element.

Kabir Edmund Helminski, *Living Presence*, Tarcher/Putnam Books.

Hazarat Inayat Khan, *The Art of Being and Becoming*, Omega.

Pir Vilayat Inayat Khan, *The Call of the Dervish*, Omega.

Spiritual Classics

* Jack Austin (editor), *The Dhammapada*, Buddhist Society.

Kahlil Gibran, *The Prophet*, Pan Books.

* Thomas à Kempis, *The Imitation of Christ*, Fount.

Brother Lawrence, *The Practice of the Presence of God*, Hodder & Stoughton.

* Juan Mascaro (translation and comment), *The Bhagavad Gita*, Penguin.

* Swami Prabhavananda and Christopher Isherwood (translation and comment), *How to Know God: The Yoga Aphorisms of Patanjali*, Vedanta Press.

Lao Tzu, *Tae Te Ching*, Penguin.

Anthologies and Encyclopedias

Igumen Chariton of Valamo, *The Art of Prayer: An Orthodox Anthology*, Faber & Faber.

Edward Conze, *Buddhist Scriptures*, Penguin.

Victor Gollancz, *The New Year of Grace*, Gollancz (out of print).

Bede Griffiths, *Universal Wisdom: A Journey Through the Sacred Wisdom of the World*, Fount.

* Rosemary Ellen Guiley, *Harper's Encyclopedia of Mystical and Paranormal Experience*, HarperCollins.
Mary Strong, *Letters of the Scattered Brotherhood*, James Clark (out of print).
R.C. Zaehner (translation), *Hindu Scriptures*, Everyman.

Universalism
Paul Brunton, *Discover Yourself* (formerly *The Inner Reality*), Weiser.
Bede Griffiths, *A New Vision of Reality*, Fount.
Aldous Huxley, *The Perennial Philosophy*, Triad.

Alternative Perspectives on Life
Carl Jung, *The Undiscovered Self*, Routledge.
J. Krishnamurti, *Freedom from the Known*, Krishnamurti Foundation.
S. Radhakrishnan, *The Creative Life*, Orient Paperbacks.
Swami Rama, *A Call to Humanity*, Himalayan Publishers.

New Science
Fritjof Capra, *The Tao of Physics*, Fontana.
David Bohm, *Wholeness and the Implicative Order*, Routledge & Kegan Paul.
Ruppert Sheldrake, *A New Science of Life*, Tarcher.

Comparative Studies
Roland Peterson, *Everyone is Right: A New Look at Comparative Religion and its Relation to Science*, DeVorss.
* Roger Schmidt, *Exploring Religion* (2nd edition), Wadsworth.
Frits Staal, *Exploring Mysticism: A Methodological Essay*, University of California Press.
R.C. Zaehner, *Hindu and Muslim Mysticism*, Oneworld.

Religious Studies
Julian Baldick, *Mystical Islam: an Introduction to Sufism*, I.B. Tauris.
Mircea Eliade, *Yoga: Immortality and Freedom*, Princeton University Press.
Friedhelm Hardy (editor), *The World's Religions: The Religions of Asia*, Routledge.
Nyanaponika Thera, *The Heart of Buddhist Meditation*, Weiser.
Evelyn Underhill, *Mysticism: The Nature and Development of Spiritual Consciousness* (12th edition), Oneworld.

* David M. Wulff, *Psychology of Religion: Classic and Contemporary Views*, John Wiley & Son.

Titles which are currently out of print may be found in good secondhand bookshops.

Two Recommended Bookshops in England

The Inner Bookshop
(new, secondhand and reduced)
111 Magdalen Road
Oxford
OX4 1RQ
Tel: 01865 245301

Watkins Books
(new and secondhand)
19 Cecil Court
London
WC2N 4EZ
Tel: 0171 836 2182

To receive information on current exercise and lecture tapes by Glyn Edwards, or music tapes by Sadhana (Santoshan and Terry Rogers), send an SAE to: S. Wollaston, 33 Cobden Road, London, E11 3PE.

To order Swami Dharmānanda Saraswati's, *Breath of Life: Breathing for Health, Vitality and Meditation*, write to: Anne Needham, Millview, Brightlingsea Road, Thorrington, Essex, CO7 8JL.

For further information on the development of mediumship and healing write to: The Secretary of the Education Committee, c/o The Spiritualists' National Union, Redwoods, Stansted Hall, Stansted, Essex, CM24 8UD.